Sound Bites of Protest

Sound Bites of Protest

Yvonne Scruggs-Leftwich
Foreword by Dorothy I. Height

Third World Press
Chicago

Third World Press
Publishers since 1967
Chicago

First Edition
Printed in the United States of America

Cover and inside text layout designer: Relana Johnson
Editor: Solomohn Ennis

Library of Congress Cataloging-in-Publication Data

Scruggs-Leftwich, Yvonne.
  Sound bites of protest / Yvonne Scruggs-Leftwich. — 1st ed.
     p. cm.
  Includes bibliographical references and index.
  ISBN-13: 978-0-88378-272-9
  ISBN-10: 0-88378-272-3
1. African American women—Social conditions. 2. African American
political activists—History—20th century. 3. African American
leadership. 4. African Americans—Civil rights. 5. African
Americans—Politics and government—20th century. 6. United States—Race
relations—History. I. Title.
  E185.86.S37 2008
  305.800973—dc22

13 12 11 10 09 08   6 5 4 3 2 1

Photos on cover (L–R):
YSL delivering keynote speech at the Annual U.S. Library of Congress.

Archbishop Desmond Tutu.

YSL being appointed to the Cabinet position of New York State Commissioner
of Housing and Community Renewal.

ACKNOWLEDGMENTS

Role models come in all genders, colors, and ages. To the extent that we fail to acknowledge this, to this extent also do we fail to acknowledge the richness of life.

Always within my view, in my ear and over my shoulders, have been my immediate family—vigilant that I not lose my focus through some trip along a tributary of outrage or passionate advocacy. They have read, individually and sometimes in groups, umpteen drafts of one or another of the essays published here, and many, many more which have not been included. My husband of twenty-five years, Rev. Edward V. Leftwich; our daughters and son, Cathryn D. Perry, Geneva-Rebecca Scruggs Perry Glickstein; Tienne D. Leftwich-Davis; and Edward V. Leftwich III, along with my brother, Leonard A. Scruggs Jr., and my sisters Harriet A. Scruggs and Roslyn E. Scruggs, constantly promote my work, from time to time differing with me and ducking, but continuing to own me anyhow.

In-laws, surrogates and sister- and brother-friends challenge me and give me candid feedback regularly: Mitchell Glickstein, Megan Pulliam, Lalita Bickers-Perrin, Gypsy Gallardo, Professor Sally A. Ross, Norman McConnery, my ninety-seven-year-old aunt Dr. Anna B. Wheaton, and my close cousin Dr. Ann Y. Eastman Tyler, fill out the voices in the family chorus. Grandsons Hunter Perry Glickstein, Avery Paul Davis and James Edward Horn make my heart sing with their pride in my work.

Finally, my long-suffering, young, highly skilled and gracious editor, Solomohn Ennis of Third World Press, is responsible for many jump-starts and rail switches to keep this book-train moving along the main track. I am deeply indebted to her.

Following is a list of persons who have profoundly influenced my writing and protesting life:

Isabel Allende	June Jordan
James Baldwin	Rev. Martin Luther King Jr., Ph.D.
Gwendolyn Brooks	Rev. Dr. Joseph E. Lowery
Eleanor Clift	Haki R. Madhubuti, Ph.D.
Jonetta Beatsch Cole, Ph.D.	Professor William R. Meek
Ellis Cose	Howard E. Mitchell, Ph.D.
L. Alan Curtis, Ph.D.	Toni Morrison
Professor Angela Y. Davis	Professor W. Sherman Perry
Horace G. Dawson, Ph.D.	Anna Quindlen
Joan Didion	Charles A. Ray, Ph.D.
Maureen Dowd	Carl Rowan
Marian Wright Edelman, Esq.	Phyllipa Schuyler
John Hope Franklin, Ph.D.	Geneva Ellen Byrd Scruggs
Betty Friedan	Lawson Andrew Scruggs, M.D.
Jewelle Taylor Gibbs, Ph.D.	Leonard Andrew Scruggs, Sr.
Senator Fred Harris	William "Bill" Tatum
Dr. Dorothy I. Height	Alice Walker
Bob Herbert	R. Joyce Whitley
bell hooks, Ph.D.	Roger Wilkins, Esq.
Molly Ivins	Patricia Williams, Esq.
Vernon Jarrett	Dean Paul Ylvisaker
Phillip E. Jones, Ph.D.	

Contents

FOREWORD

Throughout the history of African American leadership, both women and men leaders alike have given a very high priority to the written word. They have always exhorted their followers to become readers who, through educating themselves, would then be able to experience a world beyond imagination. They have always seen the written word as vital to effectively challenging the injustice of their personal or community's circumstance. And by writing to every possible audience who might be able to provide relief from our oppression, African American leaders have always demonstrated that "agitate, agitate, agitate"—in the words of Frederick Douglass—requires a march across the pages of the public's consciousness, as well as a march down the avenues and boulevards of the public agenda, using the written word.

Throughout history, also, although the literary power of African American women leaders dates at least as far back as the eighteenth century when Phyllis Wheatley wrote of her profound aspirations and elegant visions, black women have struggled constantly to have their written voices heard. Their success has been greater in fiction than in social commentary. Finding vehicles for the dissemination of their commentary and opinion remains difficult, in part because "opinion" as a legitimate province of women—black or white—has gained acceptance only just recently during my own lifetime. Given black people's history of having to scale taller obstacles than others in pursuit of equal access, it is not difficult to imagine how much further behind

African American women still lag, as the cultural currents of opinion publishers slowly have shifted.

It is axiomatic that the African American woman has been most honestly reflected in the images which she has painted with her own words. She, better than anyone, has integrated the legacy of centuries of experiences, virtually unknown to others who are **not** black women, into a rebuttal of contemporary challenges. The essays that appear in *Sound Bites of Protest* have been written in that time-honored tradition of African American women speaking for ourselves and writing our own interpretations of our experiences. Dr. Yvonne Scruggs-Leftwich says that she is "proudly guided" by the old African proverb:

"Until Lions have their own historians, tales of the hunt will always glorify the hunter."

Beginning with a rich heritage from her writer-educator ancestors, through her professional life as a public policy architect and provocateur at the local, state and national levels, to her long term position of responsibility as official analyst and advocate for contemporary civil and human rights issues on behalf of the venerable Black Leadership Forum, Inc., she has used the pen as her sword of intervention. Dr. Scruggs-Leftwich demonstrates, in one quote after another, that we, as African American women, know and tell our own story better and more clearly than anyone else.

Because Dr. Scruggs-Leftwich has been published through mainstream vehicles, this also is evidence that her perspective offers a unique view of events, whose conventional interpretation often has been otherwise. Dr. Scruggs-Leftwich's op-eds and essays have been published by such mainstream media as *Women's E-News*, the *Atlanta Journal Constitution*, the *LA Times*, the *New York Daily News* and *Chicago Tribune*, as well as in numerous editions of weekly and specialized press—especially the black press which she venerates for its commitment to featuring black writers. So, the actual role of black women—in the criminal justice system, or in the ascendancy of our people up the political career ladder, or even the unappreciated and marginalized roles which black women often have played in the power struggle for black equality—all find accurate expression when voiced through her words of unrelenting candor.

I have worked with this author over many years, largely on the issues of black leadership and African-American women's and men's occasions, about the urgency of the same concerns about which she has written here. I have heard her articulate the same commanding challenge to black women, to break free from the pack and seize the torch of leadership, in our families, in our neighborhoods and communities, and in the halls of politics and of legislative action. Yvonne Scruggs-Leftwich practices what she preaches and writes.

Dorothy I. Height
President Emerita
National Council of Negro Women

INTRODUCTION

What This Book Intends

This is an intellectual memoir, a chronicle of written thought and protest about specifically debilitating indignities—against African Americans, other people of color, women, and poor folks which have plagued me throughout my life. While this book of essays is only a small selection of the protest campaigns which I have chosen to wage or to join over the years, it is an accurate sampling of the deep concerns which have shaped my efforts, guided my energies and inspired my professional choices for as long as I can remember. So in a most profound way, these essays, speeches and articles are as relevant to the fabric of my life and the course of my actions, as any more idiosyncratically *"personal narrative of lived-through experiences,"* (Webster's Dictionary definition of "memoir") might be for someone else.

I have lived a robust life—both in fact and in thought. It is not surprising, therefore, that what I have written and present here is almost a stream-of-consciousness record of what has always gone on around me, as well as within my spirit and my head.

It seemed to be time, therefore, to gather in one place these mental artifacts and (sometimes) relics of a proactive, provocative life. Given the large volume of things which I have written over the years, it made more sense to me—and also to my insightful, editor, Solomohn Ennis—to choose a representative sample of some persistent themes from that larger body of work, rather than to be collectively exhaustive by including everything.

This latter inclusiveness risked the book's becoming overwhelmingly tiresome, a fate which I hope that I have avoided in the final streamlined version which follows...but maybe not! In any event, it also is my hope that this sample will be exclusive enough to be exciting, and catholic enough to reflect my core values and full range of intellectual concerns.

Although I have written since childhood, the ability to channel this obsession actually emerged as I became undergraduate editor-in-chief of the award-winning newspaper, *The Campus Echo*, at the HBCU (Historically Black Colleges and Universities) North Carolina Central University, then known as North Carolina College at Durham. My op-eds and editorials from that era presaged things to come. Different ways in which I have worked and lived offered broader opportunities for me to comment thoughtfully, often with ardor, about persistent conditions of servitude and marginalization lived by African Americans, women and poor people, which continue even today.

These equity, justice and political themes, which repeat throughout *Sound Bites of Protest*, have galvanized my actions along many vectors: choice of career; choice of employment; choice of volunteerism and choice of essays for this book. The four categories presented: "Articles and Commentary," "Media Essays," "Speeches and Public Addresses," and "Biographies" best organize the essays which appear here. The biographies are especially precious to me, because they are my celebration of the lives of a few of the women who have influenced me and enriched my perspectives. Some of them have passed on but their legacy continues to require that I speak often and powerfully to benefit those who frequently are unable to have their issues heard.

More significantly, these biographies copy exactly a standard set more than a century ago, in 1893, by my paternal grandfather, Dr. Lawson

Andrew Scruggs, the author of, *Women Of Distinction: Remarkable In Works And Invincible In Character. Women of Distinction* is the very first known collection of biographies about African American women by *anyone*, let alone by an African American man, has inspired me, my writing and the trajectory of my life ever since my first encounter with this phenomenal 382-page book.

Plans for its re-issue by Third World Press are reaching conclusion. The "Preface" which I have written for that new edition makes clear that the obscurity to which this remarkable peon to black women historically has been assigned, except for the recognition of *Women of Distinction* by a few scholars, must be ended. I have written in the "Preface":

> Women of Distinction was an unprecedented book when it first was published in 1893. It celebrated the accomplishments and talents of women who excelled against almost insuperable odds. Yet, in Grandfather Scruggs's words, they offered the best possible models of:

> *...Afro-American Mothers and Daughters who...endeavored to be faithful to what they understood to be the Principles of Truth and Virtue, and...who...assiduously labored, as best they could, to establish an Unimpeachable character in the Womanhood of the Race.*

> For myself, my discovery of Grandfather Scruggs's book coincided with my impatience with the early feminist ideology of the 1960s...*Women of Distinction* codified the fact that our mothers and grandmothers long since had been liberated into the world of work. Specifically, I rejected the idea that black slave-women's descendents needed to be helped down from some pedestal and permitted to find themselves in the milieu of paid laborers.

I never knew Grandfather Scruggs. He died during my father's (his son's) sophomore year as a pre-medical student at Ohio State University.

The positions which I have held over the years, described in the "About the Author" section at the end of this book, largely are self-explanatory. These jobs, however, often have provided the visibility, access to information and audiences, and a validated platform from which to have my voice heard. This was a fortunate benefit of the work which is described in Dr. Height's "Foreword" as my effort to stride "...across the pages of the public's consciousness, as well as to march down the avenues and boulevards of the public agenda, with the written word."

June Jordan, in her 1985 book, *On Call: Political Essays*, expressed eloquently and exactly my own frustrations arising from that challenge to secure vehicles for my own written work:

> I am very pleased by the publication of this second set of my political writings. Several of these essays have been published previously, in national magazines. But many of them have not. Perhaps you will find it instructive to notice the have nots. Certainly I do. I am learning, first hand, about American censorship.

> In a sense, this book must compensate for the absence of a cheaper and more immediate print outlet for my two cents. If political writing by a black woman did not strike so many editors as presumptuous or simply bizarre, then perhaps this book would not be needed. Instead, I might regularly appear, on a weekly or monthly schedule, as a national columnist. But if you will count the number of black women with regular and national forums for their political ideas, and the ideas of their constituency, you will comprehend the politics of our exclusion.

I have counted five black women who, today, fit June Jordan's profile, but only three of them write for what I would describe as my constituency. As a result, I am deeply grateful to *Women's E-News*, the electronic weekly magazine, for which I have been a commentator since the turn of this century, and where several of these essays were published first.

Also, I am very fortunate to have become a Third World Press author, which places me in the company of some notoriously and eloquently blunt advocates for the same constituency to which I proudly belong. But June Jordan's rejection of the silence to which liberal black women's voices have been relegated, precluding us from the venues where everyone, not just people of color, can listen and hear, is my lament also. Thus, the theme of serious political empowerment, analysis and advocacy for change, threads through all of my work, and especially that portion which is presented here.

Some Thoughts on The Essays' Themes

There is too much conventional wisdom having currency these days about how much better everything has gotten since "back in the day." Since I grew up and actually lived "back in the day"—in both the North and the South—I know that to be an exaggeration: often no more than wishful thinking at most, and cynical revisionist history at least. Everything is relative.

Today's instant-society too often arrives at the conclusion of "enough already" about non-mainstream issues like race, gender, and poverty; while losing sight of some continuing harsh realities. When I went away to college, traveling from my parents' Niagara Frontier home, smack on the Canadian border, to the Deep South of North Carolina, I had to get off of the train at midnight in Washington, D.C., and walk back the length of the railroad platform, to board the trains "colored car" in steerage with the caboose. Thus, "back in the day" is more than a memory for me, as fresh as the smell of wet paint in my nose and as sharp in my mind's eye as the vision of that old indignity.

In rational historic terms, these practices are too recent to *be* history. Whatever progress toward equality and justice that this nation has experienced has been primarily through changes around the edges of ordinary black folks lives and a recalibration of the weapons of destruction to make their technology more accurate. As with all cosmic shifts, movement away from blatant bigotry and racial animus is gradual, but the center of inequality continues to hold.

The matter is one of differences in the "then-and-now" experiences: subtle variations in the symbolic 2007 hanging of lynching nooses in Jena, Louisiana, which generated inequitable consequences, and the more brutal but traditionally racist, 2000 lynching of James Byrd who was dragged many miles behind a pick-up truck in Jessup, Texas, and decapitated in the process. W. Griffin's 1916 minstrel black-faced, racist hit movie, *The Birth of a Nation*, finds contemporary expression in the September 2007 ignorant and racially charged blathering of media Host Bill O'Reilly after his recent visit to Sylvia's, Manhattan/ Harlem's world-famous, venerable black-owned restaurant. He went there as the guest of Rights Leader Rev. Al Sharpton.

O'Reilly reported that he, "couldn't get over the fact that there was no difference between the black-run restaurant and others (restaurants) in New York City. ...There wasn't any kind of craziness at all."

He told listeners that his grandmother—and many other white Americans—feared blacks because they didn't know any and are swayed by violent images in black culture. Of course, any images of black culture which are seen by white people who don't actually know any blacks, in all probability are the product of network media, programmed and produced by white people.

In other words, O'Reilly and his ignorant network who know nothing of the diversity and richness of twenty-first century black culture still think, in effect, that African Americans wear loin cloth, and when dining out, eat with their hands and swing from the chandeliers while scratching under their arms; residual images from movies like *The Birth of a Nation* and the painfully enduring "Tarzan" sequels. It is clear that O'Reilly does not understand this perspective and therefore, he offends, and will continue to do so.

Worthy efforts to educate all Americans about each other have been short, sweet and largely, have died aborning. I wrote a few years ago in the newspaper *Newsday*, that:

> The Clinton race initiative demonstrated that, until there is clarity about the grievances that diversely situated Americans harbor about race, there can be no meaningful modification of the practices that are perceived as racist. We learned from the single year of the Race Initiative that, contrary to conventional wisdom, very few Americans have any substantive knowledge about the four centuries of black people's evolution from the seventeenth century's brutally imported slaves to today's growing cadre of enfranchised and socially, economically and politically ascendant African Americans. ...

> The (Clinton-sponsored) town meetings began to diminish parochialism and expose ignorant misperceptions, not only about African Americans, but about other erroneously undifferentiated ethnic categories

of hyphenated Americans: Native-Americans, Latino/Hispanic-Americans; Southeast Asian and Pacific Rim-Americans, and other peoples of color and ethnic or religious diversity who are far less homogeneous and monolithic than so called conventional wisdom suggests.

Too bad that the Race Initiative was over before O'Reilly's fifteen minutes of Andy Warhol fame started. He might have learned something useful.

Other recent instances of persistent and even more deadly bigotry abound. For example, the 2006 degradation in the largely black Gulf of Mexico communities of Louisiana, Mississippi and Alabama as a result of hurricanes Katrina and Rita, is ranging from the malignant, "benign neglect" concepts which mimic the designs for "Negro removal" offered by cynical 1950s and 60s urban renewal planners and social engineers, to the felonious racial profiling and assaults by all levels of governments on human beings, mostly black and poor. These assaults include aggressive acts by the law enforcement and criminal justice systems against black men who are actually disabled, disoriented and simply displaced by the hurricane disasters.

Today's political engineering in the Gulf region—especially New Orleans—is mirroring Florida's 2000 presidential election's torch-burn-and-plunder assault on black voters and exemplifies what I had in mind when I wrote in 2001:

> To the utter dismay of many, strident voices have insisted that votes cast by American citizens don't count and should not be counted. The very suggestion of this disenfranchisement stirs creeping feelings of recidivism into a dark bigoted past of voter intimidation and blatant denial of voting

rights to black Americans. This in not paranoia. It is an enlightened self-interested application of history's lessons.

...In the African American experience, it takes no quantum leap from a willful decision to disregard thousands of voters' ballots, made by the notoriously arbitrary deep south State of Florida, to other all too familiar and unilateral actions denying voters their constitutional franchise. Blacks recognize the pattern. We have lived it time and time again when... others have used spurious reasons and transparent conspiratorial methods to trash African American votes.

"Deny My Vote Today and They'll
Come for Yours in The Morning" (2001)

Translation: If black voters fail to return home to the Gulf, the balance of political power in that entire majority-black region returns to *status quo ante:* blacks will no longer be a political force with which to be reckoned. So much for the 1964 Civil Rights Act's and 1965 Voting Rights Act's gains as practical tools for equality and justice in the Gulf Region. The troubling delay in post-hurricane rebuilding in urban communities of the Gulf Coast, principally New Orleans, has been facilitated directly by the failure of the Federal government to have a viable national urban policy. It is not as though there has never been a Federal admission of responsibility for guaranteeing access to affordable housing and to urban economic investment which preserved the egalitarian tradition of cities.

In my recent book, *Consensus and Compromise: Creating the First National Urban Policy Under President Carter* (University Press of America 2006,) I wrote passionately and poignantly about the foregone opportunity for national political governmental leadership to assure the viability of America's cities. If that first 1979 Congressionally enacted Urban Policy had been implemented at all, today's cynical manipulation of developers' access and "wired" incentives, designed to benefit only the rich and privileged residents of New Orleans, would not be acceptable or even possible. Specifically I stated in the book's "Preface":

> The first official 'National Urban Policy ...was created during a time when Congress and federal agency appointees were actually troubled by the dim prospects for 'cities in distress,' in contrast with today's slash-and-burn, scorched-earth use of Federal power. As a consequence, the (Fed's) policies sought to provide public relief, not to the richest among us, but to identifiable distressed cities where most of the poorest among us lived. Public appointees consciously sought to meet the challenge of high-minded standards of personal and public performance:

> Please make sure that the urban policy statement leads off with a position on the poor and black of our cities, and how the first aim of an urban policy should be to transform this group into a stable community with dependable and adequate income, social equality and racial mobility.
> —HUD's Assistant Secretary,
> Robert C. Embry, Esq. (1977)

Public servants at all levels of government who are responsible for New Orleans' currently unrelieved post-Katrina distress, should be forcibly inoculated with values, like Bob Embry's, which prevailed when the 1979 National Urban Policy was created.

Chapters 7 and 14 "Imus's Demise Must Herald New Standards" and "Hardcore Rap Does Not Deserve A Constitutional Shield" offer continuing examples of verbal racial lynching and misogynist trash talking, ranging from gangsta' gutter labels for women in general, to Don Imus's racial slurs against Rutgers University's winning women basketball players, in particular. These and other regular offenses speak volumes about how little actually has changed in the treatment of black women by men, black and white. They remind us of how much work still needs to be done—among both women and men—to permanently stop this abuse, and render it extinct.

The general claim that the United States is a successful multi-racial civil society and that, as a nation, we are committed to racial and gender justice—on the ground as well as in the breech—is a very new work in progress, begun barely a quarter-of-a-century ago. My mission in what I have written always has been to guarantee that everyone continues to do this hard work on justice and fairness; that this nation—my country—not rest on its laurels, there being too few of these for such a perch to be comfortable; and above all, that America should not to be smug, superior or self-righteous, emphasized throughout the book, but especially in Chapters 17 and 19 "Always Look a Gift Horse in the Mouth: Things are Not Always as They Seem" and "A Passion for Progress and Parity." God is not finished with this county yet.

Chapter 4, "Black and Latina Women Locked in the Jail House and the Poor House," was inspired by young women of color like Kemba Smith, the innocent young black college student who summarily was found guilty for her association with her drug-involved, dead at the time of her sentencing, boyfriend. At twenty-four years old, having no pertinent information with which to bargain with prosecutors for her freedom because she knew nothing, Kemba Smith was sentenced to twenty-four years in prison by a drug obsessed criminal justice system. Her draconian fate echoing the fate of countless black women throughout history, powerless to speak effectively for themselves.

Dr. Dorothy I. Height's foreword to this book reminds me of the iconic value of black women's speaking out and speaking for ourselves. The late Mrs. Mary McLeod Bethune was the founder and first president of the National Council of Negro Women (NCNW). Dr. Height, who now has led NCNW for over fifty years, tells the story that Mrs. Bethune asked First Lady Eleanor Roosevelt to deliver a response for her to President Franklin Delano Roosevelt's message which he had sent to Mrs. Bethune by his wife. The President had indicated that he preferred having a white man advance the cause of African Americans rather than to appoint a "Negro" person to the White House staff for that purpose. The President felt that invectives advanced or spoken by white people on behalf of "the Negro" would have more agency and greater credibility with the larger mainstream community than would his appointment of the African American, Frank Horn, whom Mrs. Bethune had suggested. Her reply was: "With all due respect, Mr. President, that may be true, but no one can better speak for me than I can speak for myself."

This is a powerful expression of self-esteem. I wish that I thought this always to be true. I wish that people who are marginalized and discriminated against and prevented from having access to entitled benefits from this society regularly were able and willing—especially today in the repressive climate of faux patriotism and harsh economic stratification and elitism—to express the frustrations and pain of such bias, disrespect and dishonor at the time that their indignities occur. Unfortunately, that course of action often has been fatal in black's history and anyway, usually has been unavailable to African Americans in too many venues, without the threat of loss of life and/or treasure.

The Nature of My Crucible
Born during the great Depression, a Yankee in Niagara Falls, New York, and socialized within the values of well-educated and racially

aggressive ancestors and immediate family, I was a receptive vessel for the challenges of activism and advocacy. My parents were life members of the NAACP (National Association for the Advancement of Colored People). The NAACP's *Crisis Magazine,* founded and guided by Walter White and W.E.B Du Bois was the first subscription magazine that I remember being regularly present in our home. I read it and learned. Both parents held leadership positions in a number of social benefit organizations, including the Elks, various Free Masonry organizations for both men and women, social change movements and unions, and also, within the African American church.

A vivid memory of Mother, who was a teacher when I was small, before becoming involved in partisan politics, is my awe as I trailed, in tow, behind her endless marches down two blocks to the corner where Public School No. 75 was located. She went to school whenever I reported any infraction of my code of entitlement to fair treatment—and in this school where all of the teachers were white and there were zero African American full-time teachers, there were numerous infractions.

Therefore, we took many, many "marches for fairness" which I came to call them. My mother was afraid of nothing, deferred to no earthly being and was smarter than most people. She was the black community's "go-to-person" when things went strange in "Up-South" Buffalo, New York.

Mother would blanch at today's interpretation of Lincoln Republicanism, the party to which both Mother and Daddy belonged and from which Mother ran for significant public offices in the 1940s and 50s. She seconded Thomas Dewey's nomination for Governor when the Statewide Republican Party convened in Saratoga Springs, New York and I attended that convention with her. I loved the racetrack where the sulkies ran at Saratoga but I remember nothing much about the convention—other than that I was there.

I can visualize today my mother sitting on the dais before the Convention's general body. She and her best friend, Bertha J. Diggs, New York State's first African American State Director (Commisioner) of Labor and Employment, were terrific images; in their suits, bright white gloves and smart cloche hats. They were the only black, and as I recall, surely, the only African American women on the Dais.

I hung out with Daddy when he went to buy the Sunday newspaper and stopped off at the local Ice Cream and conversation parlor, The Sugar Bowl. He talked religion and politics with his male friends and exposed me to the model of Black men of gravitas and civic authority and knowledge. His metre was not political but fraternal. Daddy held closed-door sessions with students and leaders of Masonry—from the Blue House through the Consistory to the Shriners. I used to try to eavesdrop with my ear to a heating vent which opened into the next room of his closed door study. But when I could not make much sense of what I heard of this "secret society" murmuring, I got bored and stopped. He was head of the Deacon's and Usher's Boards variously in the Baptist Church.

Mother, ever an independent soul, was educated in Episcopal schools including St. Paul's College. She never left that denomination. and finally, after her loss of patience with what the Republican Party was becoming, she turned her attention back to the church and became one of the first women members in the 1970s of the New York State Vestry— the church's governing board.

These were my very first role models, other later ones are listed in the "Acknowledgements" and throughout the text. But my initial determination to think for myself and to write what I think, came from my parents and their *lived-resistance* to intimidation and propaganda. They knew the "real deal" and, unlike so many blacks in their generation, they accepted no guilt for the despicable experiences which they both had suffered in their lives as a result, not only of their color and race, but also because of their fortunate educational backgrounds and their steel ideological spines.

These valued characteristics and accomplishments often led to their being labeled "uppity" and "arrogant", terms which usually were accompanied by the typical racial, ethnic and bestial slurs, intended to diminish the black people who are the targets. They never let any of their bigoted detractors see them sweat. They were great on-the-job trainers for the life which I chose and have lived.

Resources For Our Future
The appendix of this book contains a list of organizations which share the commitment to equity, justice, progress and opportunity which I have championed in the essays and speeches in *Sound Bites of Protest*. For those who actually want to do something positive for people of color, women, and poor folks, these organizations offer an excellent opportunity for pitching in and helping to bring about change.

No organization is stronger than its weakest members. In my calculus, the law of large numbers increases the possibility of accumulative strength in direct relationship to the number of people who join in to do the organization's work. There is no excuse for not making a commitment to support the work of these groups once specific information is made available for contacting, joining and/or supporting the group of your choice. The "Appendix" has useful contact information.

I believe that if you are not a part of the solution, then you are a part of the problem. Promoting racial, social, and gender justice is not a silent spectator sport.

My mother, Geneva B. Scruggs and my father, Leonard A. Scruggs, Sr., with me as I boarded the train to begin the first leg of my trip to Europe as a Fulbright Fellow.

Part One

Articles and Commentary

An Urgent Independence Struggle for African Women—Gender Matters

Millions of women in the world are living a death sentence just because in their cultures their lives do not count.

Conventional wisdom recognizes that the Fourth of July has little celebratory meaning anywhere else in the world besides the United States and, maybe in a perverted way, England. Yet, the language of the "Declaration of Independence"—written at the end of the American Revolution by Thomas Jefferson and introduced in Congress on July 4, 1776, 230 years ago—is used by Americans not only to assert who we are as a people, but is also held up to those from other countries as a standard of America's humanity to help us define ourselves to them. Especially that the Declaration's pronouncement, "...that all **men** are created equal, that they are endowed by their creator with certain unalienable Rights, that among these are Life, Liberty and the pursuit of Happiness..." is America's historic motto.

Today in the United States of America, we assert that a contemporary translation of these words from the Declaration now includes everyone and that we have pretty much gotten over the *"men"* thing in this document. However, we recognize that there is plenty of evidence that the *"independence"* thing still needs a lot of work as far as women are concerned.

In many other parts of the world, specifically in Africa, work seems not even to have begun for women on the "Life, Liberty and the pursuit of Happiness" rights. Certainly there is virtually no effective intention to "secure" their unalienable right to "Life," ...literally. During the same period when we here in the United States are celebrating Independence

Day this Fourth of July, 1500-plus women and their supporters from across the world will be meeting in Nairobi, Kenya, in memoriam of the millions of women in the world who have lost their lives to HIV/AIDS or who are living a death sentence from the pandemic disease just because in their cultures their lives do not count. From the force of their physical dehumanization in chauvinistically repressive cultures, through the economic imperative of sex-for-survival from starvation and death, to the conflict driven conversion of rape into a war-time weapon of mass destruction, African women's bodies have become the vehicles for male dominance and supremacy on the African continent and elsewhere in the developing world.

The first Global Conference on Women and AIDS, therefore, is belated yet appropriately located in Africa. It is being sponsored by what is one of the largest and oldest women's organization in the world, the World Young Women's Christian Association (World YWCA). Dr. Lorraine Cole, CEO of the YWCA USA states:

> The AIDS pandemic, particularly as it affects women, is a high priority of the World YWCA and will be the focal point during the upcoming quadrennial YWCA World Council meeting in Nairobi... Although much attention has been focused in this country on the plight of HIV and AIDS on the continent of Africa, it also is a much less well known fact that AIDS is the number one killer of young African American women between the ages of twenty-five and thirty-four... [largely] contracted ...in their teens and early twenties. Therefore, the voice of the YWCA USA on the subject of HIV and AIDS...will be crucial during the World Council meeting.

In fact, the global impact on women of HIV/AIDS will occupy the Kenyan Conference Agenda for the first three days. "Life, Liberty and

3

the Pursuit of Happiness" finds new meaning for women, American as well as African, when confronted by the death threat of the pandemic HIV/AIDS. Studies report that 54 percent of new HIV/AIDS infections occur in girls and young women, and that 80 percent of these new infections result from sex with their husbands or primary partners. Large numbers of these women live in Sub-Saharan Africa.

In most cases their lives are taken because of a death sentence held over their heads because they are women—and because, as World Human Rights Watch has repeatedly documented, most recently in late 2006, the deadly link between women's rights abuses and the spread of HIV/AIDS is slowly gaining recognition—but not before millions of women lost their lives to the disease.

Evidence indicates that women especially at risk are those in heterosexual marriages or long term unions in a society where men commonly engage in sex outside the union and women confront abuse if they demand condom use. The Human Rights Watch World Report 2006 states:

> Every day in every corner of the world, women and girls are beaten in their homes, trafficked into forced prostitution, raped by soldiers and rebels in armed conflicts, sexually abused by their 'caretakers,' deprived of equal rights to property and other economic assets, assaulted for not conforming to gender norms and often left with no option but to trade sex for survival. The relationship between abused women's rights and their vulnerability to AIDS is acutely clear in Africa, where 58 percent of those infected with HIV are women ... In Kenya, simply because of their gender, many AIDS victims sink into poverty and will die even sooner because customs condone evicting women from their home and taking their property upon [the husband's] death.

These are the same husbands whom, very often, infected the women with HIV / AIDS in the first place. They are the same husbands who, often, abused the women if they sought to protect themselves with prophylactic measures like condoms or otherwise did not conform to the gender norms and local customs of their marriages.

While Africa leads the world in HIV / AIDS incidents and deaths, many other nations are not far behind. Yale University's AIDS WATCH reports that Latin America and the Caribbean regions have the second highest rates of newly reported cases of HIV. And in the U.S., adding to the urgency of Dr. Lorraine Cole's statistics on young women, there has been an alarming up-tick in the incidents of infections reported for older American women, as in Africa, attributed to heterosexual contacts with their husbands.

From Kenya, Nobel Laureate, Dr. Wangari Maathai, a huge icon for women's empowerment throughout the developing world, not just in Kenya, reports:

> No one can underestimate the challenge that the tragedy of HIV / AIDS puts before all countries. Nowhere has the devastation been greater than in sub-Saharan Africa. Methods to alleviate the suffering and, hopefully, find a cure require our full commitment. For too long, discussing HIV / AIDS in our communities has been taboo. This must end. We must encourage free and full public debate on the threat. We must be frank about how the HIV virus spreads through unprotected sex or intravenous drug use, and how poverty and inequality between women and men are the major driving forces of the pandemic in Africa. We must also increase access to information, care and treatment. In this decisive and difficult struggle in Africa we need the critical encouragement, support and cooperation from the rest of world so that we win the battle.

The First Global Conference on Women and Aids in Nairobi in July 2007, coming more than twenty-five years after HIV/AIDS first was identified as an international scourge in 1982, is a forum which potentially may jumpstart serious action on behalf of women deemed abused and expendable, especially in Africa. But given the cultural, traditional, misogynistic and brutal barriers to women's equality worldwide, its hoped for outcome may be an exaggeration.

What realistically can occur, however, may be a heightened awareness among U.S. policymakers, forced by an increasingly informed and demanding international community, that real damage and loss of opportunity is resulting from the emphasis of President Bush's $15 Billion AIDS initiative (President's Emergency Plan for AIDS Relief—PEPFAR). The imposition of a socially conservative litmus test of the ABC strategy for the distribution and administration of PEPFAR aid, is actually a killer for African women. The Fourth of July American mantra—when imposed upon global women, translates as follows: **A**—Abstention (Pursuit of Happiness—for men only); **B**—Be Faithful (Life—death by marriage); **C**—Condoms (Liberty—a man's choice)

This simple yet factual illustration describes the current formula for curbing the African HIV/AIDS pandemic. It clearly is not the winning strategy for exporting the American values of Independence and Freedom, which we celebrate each and every July Fourth.

Black Women are Credible Presidential Candidates

African American girls and women need to see role models who demonstrate that politics is a legitimate professional aspiration with top level rewards, and that the presidency and vice-presidency are within their reach.

Sometimes an historical review of the facts places an idea about institutional change in proper perspective and better informs efforts to even the odds faced by one or another disregarded or under-represented group. Such is the case with current discussions intended to change expectations for women who have what it takes to become president and/or vice-president of the United States of America.

Of particular concern to a number of African Americans, therefore, is the omission of plausible black women from the most widely circulated lists, particularly the lists being reported by national media like *Parade* and *Harper's Bazaar* magazines. Several outstanding African American women's names are on the lists, to be sure. However, their careers clearly are not identified with elective politics. These counter-intuitive selections are then widely reported in the news media, to many who already are convinced that there are not very many credible women political leaders in the African American community.

The facts, however, tell a very different story. Black women political professionals have led the way in puncturing the glass ceiling of competitive presidential politics.

The first woman—and in fact the first African American—to contend for nomination to the presidency at a convention of either of the two major political parties was Brooklyn, New York's Congresswoman, Shirley Chisholm, who served in the House of Representative from 1969 to 1982. She ran for the presidency in 1972, assembling 151 delegate votes on the first ballot of the Democratic nominating convention held in Miami, Florida.

Her candidacy was not supported by the major feminist organization, NOW, nor by the local and Congressional Black Caucus organizations of that day, reflecting a deeply entrenched view that the time was not yet ripe for a woman, and surely not a black women, to run for the presidency. Chisholm ran anyway, ignoring them, as well as one elderly black male voter in Harlem who told her: "Young woman, what are you doing out here in this cold? Did you get your husbands breakfast this morning? Did you straighten up your house?What are you doing running for office? That is something for men!"

 A former teacher, with a master's degree, Congresswoman Chisholm held a long record of participation in Democratic Party politics. She was a member of the New York State Assembly for four years, and a leading activist in New York City politics beginning in the 1950s. She was a founding member of the Congressional Black Caucus, in addition to her provocative presence on House of Representatives standing committees.

As the first African American woman ever elected to Congress, Chisholm had name recognition as well as strong credentials as a political professional. In other words, one could not view her as entering politics laterally, or even being a stealth candidate, on a joy ride from another prominent but politically neutral profession.

Later, Dr. Leonora B. Fulani was the National Alliance Party's candidate for lieutenant governor of the State of New York in 1984. In 1988 and 1992 she was that party's nominee for the presidency. She was the first woman and first African American to appear on the presidential ballot in all fifty states, and she qualified for $2 million dollars in Federal matching funds.

Today, Dr. Fulani works as a political commentator. She is a vocal advocate, a syndicated columnist and is co-founder and official of several independent party collaboratives. She is unquestionably a political professional who has demonstrated her investment in political competition at the very highest national level. A woman still in her prime years, she has already made national history and is reported to be considering another run for the presidency.

Therefore, when the highly touted lists of potential presidential and vice-presidential candidates appear, one wonders: Where are the names of the prominent professional black women politicians like United States Senators and Congresswomen, mayors, speakers of state legislators, presidents of state senates, elected secretaries of state and gubernatorial candidates?

The list-makers appear not to be serious when they include only black women who certainly are talented in their professions, but who most certainly are not viable political candidates. But there are many African American women who do stand in powerful juxtaposition with the list's white women, who themselves are professional politicians, public political activists, and clearly realistic contenders for the White House.

For example, one important missing name is that of former U.S. Senator and Ambassador to New Zealand, Carol Moseley Braun, LLD, the first black woman in history to be elected to the U.S. Senate. Clearly in her prime years, Moseley-Braun is a lawyer who has been a U.S. Prosecutor, a ten year veteran of the Illinois State House of Representatives, and is a campaign-experienced victor as Cook County's Recorder of Deeds.

Like other listed professional women politicians who are now currently out of elective office—such as former Governor Christie Todd Whitman, former Senator and Cabinet Secretary Elizabeth Hanford Dole and former Republican Party Chairwoman Linda Lingle—former Senator and Ambassador Moseley-Braun's name should be included. She is qualified and has earned the right to inclusion.

Some list-makers have stated that naming any woman who is in an election cycle is a partisan act and therefore precluded. This appears automatically to eliminate any of the current black Congresswomen from the list. Given the two-year length of a congressional term, Congress people are always in an election cycle.

Nonetheless, the most prominent example of a woman's landmark White House run—in addition to Congresswoman Chisholm—was Congresswoman Geraldine Ferrarro. A lawyer, she served three terms in the House of Representatives immediately before her nomination to the Democratic ticket as the vice-presidential running mate with presidential nominee Walter Mondale. Thus, the emerging precedents favors—indeed requires—the inclusion of women members of the House—not just Senators—on the lists.

The White House Project, initiated in 1997, was designed to "...shift to a climate of expectancy" by making it "...commonplace for a woman to run." *Harper's Bazaar* magazine, reporting on the Project in March 1999, commented on the puzzling inclusion of a number of unlikely presidential hopefuls on the first list. The magazine observed that in the view of many who were listed, "...inclusion seemed merely a fun, ego-stroking parlor game with few real ramifications."

There was guarded recognition of this practicality in the most recent

(June 2002) addition to the White House Project's list, of House of Representatives' Minority Whip, Congresswoman Nancy Pelosi. She is an appropriate and ideal possible contender who has proven her competitive mettle. But the Project still did not list any black Congresswomen.

Yet, the Project's own expectations seem to be more serious than that. The White House Project's website and literature feature pictures of ethnically diverse young women, accompanied by the queries: "Does she think about becoming President? At what age does she decide it's impossible?" The Project's website further states: "We also need to remember that there are an increasing number of girls who are growing up seeing that women have never been president... If we want a girl of eleven or eight to be president, we have to prepare the world..." We also have to prepare the girls themselves.

The recent White House Project's collaboration on a program with The Girl Scouts of America is a step in that direction. Joining with a group like the Boys and Girls Clubs of America; for example, probably also would reach a much larger number of African American and Hispanic girls. African American girls and young women need to be presented with role models who demonstrate that politics is a legitimate professional aspiration with potentially top level rewards; that the presidency and vice-presidency are within their reach. They need to see realistic examples, of women who look like them to inspire them to choose career paths which actually will prepare them for the challenges in the political arena.

The list, as presently constructed, offers no examples of national level black women politicians whose career ladder climbs target the goal of national elected political office, although most of the white women on the same list offer such examples. Newly released data from a White House Project-sponsored study strongly supports the notion that women candidates should have strong track records as public officials; must demonstrate decisiveness in crisis situations, must have command of crucial public policy issues and must project a very tough-guy [gal] approach to getting the job done. These findings confirm that novices and the uninitiated need not apply.

Enter some of the most obviously qualified African American women candidates for the White House. Let's begin with the United States Congress.

Today there are fifteen African American women in Congress. They all demonstrate by the political careers which they have forged, almost always against heavy opposition, that running for office, getting elected and governing are their primary career goals. If one uses the same standards to measure black women's potential for successful competition for top political office as the Projects' study found apply to white women candidates—there were no African Americans or other women of color included in the Project's study—these Congressional Black Caucus (CBC) members rise to the top like cream.

Some concrete examples are provided by the four women presently in CBC leadership positions and who occupy its most senior ranks:

CBC Chairwoman, Eddie Bernice Johnson, became a Member of Congress in 1993. She is from Houston, Texas. Not only has she been victorious over male competitors in winning the CBC post, but she was the first African American women to ever win elected public office in Dallas, Texas, when, in 1972, she began her tenure in the Texas House of Representatives. In 1986, she again became the first African American since Reconstruction to be elected to the Texas State Senate. She holds professional, bachelor's and master's degrees, from Notre Dame, Texas Christian and Southern Methodist Universities, the latter in Public Administration.

Earlier this year Congresswoman Johnson organized and led the first-ever retreat of a coalition from all ethnic congressional caucuses—Hispanic, Asian and black—for a week of dialogue and strategy development. Additionally, she has created a Global Accord of Women for World Peace, one of the first of its kind organized by an elected American leader.

Johnson headed a delegation of CBC members to the World Conference Against Racism (WCAR), held in Durban, South Africa, originally as a U.S. delegate. When the U.S. government aborted this country's official WCAR participation, Congresswoman Johnson's leadership had already supported the credentialling of the seven CBC members through the Black Leadership Forum's NGO Delegation to WCAR, which facilitated their highly visible leadership throughout the entire conference.

CBC's Second Vice-Chair, Sheila Jackson Lee, LLD, a Member of Congress since 1995, is an attorney who holds a Yale University undergraduate degree and a law degree from the University of Virginia. She has had a long political career, including her 1990 At-Large election to the Houston, Texas City Council as the first African American women to serve in this capacity.

Both a lawyer in private practice and later a partner in a Houston law firm, Jackson Lee also served as Associate Judge for the City of Houston. She was staff counsel to the U.S. House of Representatives and Select

Committee on Assassinations from 1977–1978. As a member of the House Judiciary Committee, she was a prominent and vocal presence during the 1996 Presidential Impeachment hearings.

Congresswoman Maxine Waters, has been a Member of Congress since 1991, representing Los Angeles, California. With high national name recognition as a fierce defender of the most disregarded and disenfranchised, Waters is a fearlessly persistent over-seer of excesses and abuses of governmental power and a strong defender of Constitutional protections. She has focused on economic and community development and been a persistent voice in the debates on illegal drug interdiction and governmental responsibility.

She is a former Chairperson of the Congressional Black Caucus and has had a fourteen-year career in the California State Assembly, where she became Democratic Caucus Chair. She earned a bachelor's degree from California State University.

Congresswoman Eleanor Holmes Norton, LLD, has been a Delegate to Congress from the District of Columbia since 1991, where she has led fights for government reform, fiscal solvency, equal rights, women's rights, voting rights and statehood rights for D.C. She is a Yale Law School graduate of respected national reputation, and has also earned a master's degree from Yale.

Norton was named one of the 100 most important American women in a recent national survey. She chaired the U.S. Equal Opportunity Commission under President Jimmy Carter, has served on the boards of several Fortune 500 companies and prestigious foundations, and headed professional associations of legal governance.

The eleven other African American women Members of Congress also are superbly qualified and obviously committed to their political careers. In order of their seniority, they are:

Congresswoman Eva Clayton, from North Carolina, whose term began in 1992. She is the first African American woman to serve from her state. During the eight years prior, Clayton served on the Warren County Board of Commissioners. She holds both bachelor's and master's degrees, from her states Johnson C. Smith and North Carolina Central Universities, respectively.

Congresswoman Corrine Brown, representing Florida's Third District since 1993, is one of the first two post-Reconstruction women elected to Congress from her state. She had previously served in the Florida House of Representatives for ten years, and holds both bachelor's and master's degrees from Florida A& M University.

Congresswoman Carrie Pittman Meek, Florida's other first post-Reconstruction women elected in 1993, also served from 1979 until 1992 in the State legislature and senate. Retiring from Congress after this current term, she has mentored a son who is a candidate for her seat in the November 2002 election. Congresswoman Meek holds Florida A&M University bachelor's and University of Michigan master's degrees.

Congresswoman Cynthia Ann McKinney, also elected to Congress in 1993, from a congressional district which was subsequently re-districted into one of the most ethnically diverse districts in Georgia. She was still re-elected after redistricting by a persuasive margin. She previously served in the Georgia state legislature from 1988 to 1992. She holds a bachelor's degree and is completing her Master's degree in International Relations from Tufts University's Fletcher School of Law and Diplomacy.

Congresswoman Juanita Millender-McDonald, elected in 1996, is the first woman from California's Thirty-seventh District to serve in Congress. She previously served several years in the California State Assembly and was subsequently the first African American elected to the Carson City Council where her colleagues selected her to serve as Mayor Pro Tempore. She holds both bachelor's, master's and post-graduate credentials from the University of the Redlands and California State University.

Congresswoman Julia Carson, the first woman and the first African American elected to Congress by the people of Indianapolis, Indiana in 1996. For the previous eighteen years, she had served in the Indiana General Assembly and Senate, and also was elected to Indiana's Citizen Legislature. In 1990, she was elected to a six year term as Trustee for Center Township of Marion County. She is an extraordinary grass-roots leader whose personal odyssey has made her an immensely popular role model for achievement and self-actualization.

Congresswoman Donna Christian-Christensen, M.D., in 1996 she became the first woman Delegate from the Virgin Islands and is the first woman physician ever to serve in Congress. She also is the first woman to represent an offshore Territory. Born in New Jersey, she has served as Democratic National Committeewoman, Democratic Territorial Committee member, and gas been a Convention Delegate since 1984 and Platform Committee member since 1988. She holds degrees from Notre Dame University and George Washington University's School of Medicine.

Congresswoman Carolyn Cheeks Kilpatrick, was elected from Michigan's fifteenth congressional district in 1996, after an eighteen-year career as the State House of Representative's member from Detroit.

The State House seat which she vacated in 1996 was immediately won by the son whom she mentored, Honorable Kwame Kilpatrick, who has now become Detroit's mayor. Congresswoman Kilpatrick has earned degrees from Ferris State University and Western Michigan University and holds a master's degree from the University of Michigan.

Congresswoman Barbara Lee, was elected in 1998 to fill her mentor's seat, seasoned Congressman Ron Dellums from California's Oakland District, she has continued a career of public political service which began when she became a congressional intern for the District from which she subsequently was elected. She served in the California State Assembly from 1990 to 1996, and in the State Senate from 1996 to 1998. She holds a Mills College bachelor's degree and a Master's in Social Work from the University of California at Berkeley. She has high name recognition for her courageous peace advocacy stand following the September 11, terrorist attack.

Stephanie Tubbs Jones, LLD, is the first African American to be elected, in 1999, to represent Ohio's eleventh congressional district which serves East Cleveland and the inner-ring suburbs. A graduate of Case Western Reserve University's Law School, she served previously as the first woman and first African American Cuyahoga County Prosecutor. She was also the first woman Common Pleas Judge in the County and was a Cleveland Municipal Court Judge. Her bachelor's degree is also from Case Western.

Congresswoman Diane E. Watson, Ph.D. was the United States Ambassador to the Federated States of Micronesia from 1998 until her term as representative for Los Angeles, California's thirty-second congressional district began in 2001. The first African American woman elected to the L.A. Board of Education in 1975, she then was elected to a five-term, twenty-year incumbency as California State Senator, which ended in 1998. She holds bachelor's, master's and doctoral degrees from the University of California, California State, and Claremont Graduate University.

This list is just a tip of the iceberg. It documents some of the many highly competitive, decisive, laser-focused and tough African American women who stand in the penumbra of a potential presidential nomination. More detailed information about these and other outstanding African American women in the profession of national politics is available from the *Congressional Black Caucus Foundation's Directory 107th Congress: 2001–2002*, and from LaVerne McCain Gill's rich study, *African American Women in Congress: Forming and Transforming History* (Rutgers University Press).

Ward Connerly is Not Colorblind: He is Just Blind and Dangerous

The myth of the browning of America is grossly distorted.

Ward Connerly, California's affluent, black Anti-affirmative Action hired gun, is up to his old tricks of pretending that race does not matter. He is godfather to the Racial Privacy Initiative, which, if passed by California's Legislature, would forbid state agencies from making any entry in agency records indicating the race of an African-, Latino-, Asian- or Native- American seeking to access public benefits. The alleged purpose of the Initiative is to expunge the records of all diverse cultural identities because its supporters believe that this will melt prejudice and racism quickly—at least in California.

Many Americans disagree however, seeing this effort as misguided, simply cynical, at least naive, and most certainly dead wrong. Here are six reasons why:

1. Data about race provide concrete evidence for litigation against discrimination and inequity. Since before the 1954 Supreme Court case, *Brown v. Board of Education* which nullified the separate-but-equal doctrine of segregation in public education, hard data has been the foundation of successful constitutional challenges on behalf of civil rights. In all subsequent equal access cases, race data has provided tangible proof that one race got fewer of public benefits than another race.

For example, following the Supreme Court's 1995 anti-Affirmative Action decision in *Hopwood v. State of Texas*, the use of race data confirmed a precipitous drop in blacks entering the University of Texas

19

Law School, from the year before *Hopwood* to one student the year after. Without race data, the deleterious impact of *Hopwood* on black-access would be unknown. Moreover, in studies in 2002 on housing discrimination, race data has clearly confirmed that African Americans pay more for their homes, receive less favorable mortgage rates and continue to be disproportionately concentrated in segregated enclaves. Academies of Science's report, "Measuring Housing Discrimination in a National Study," confirms continuing problems of racial discrimination. The Study was based on an analysis of the data linking race to home purchases, to mortgage availability, and to illegal steering of home buyers in order to maintain patterns of racial concentration and exclusion. These practices cause blacks to fail in their efforts to own homes, to pay more for the homes which they purchase, to receive less favorable mortgages and higher interest rates, and to continue to live in segregated enclaves. In short, data about race are the basis for legal actions to protect minorities and preserve civil rights.

2. *A " don't ask / don't tell" race policy will not make racism go away.* For too long, African Americans have been sent blunt signals that being black is undesirable, that blackness is a reason for shame and that asserting pride in African racial and cultural identity was a form of trouble-making which should be stifled. The Racial Privacy Initiative simply seeks to convert these negative messages into state law: e.g., it will be better for everyone if no one asks and no one tells anything about race. Thus, the victims of racial discrimination once again are being blamed for bringing up the embarrassing subject of their race. Moreover, bigots are being given a guilt-free pass, since data substantiating their discriminatory behavior would not be available under the Racial Privacy Proposal.

3. *Race explains the richness of American cultural diversity and it should be*

celebrated, not hidden. Soul food, jazz, egg rolls, fried rice, tortillas, and the Latin beat were all created in a "color blind" America, right? That notion is as silly as it sounds. Moreover, as increasing numbers of white Americans are finally releasing their Native American ancestors from their family closets of skeletons, the Racial Privacy proposal insists that all of these race-based sources of cultural richness, diversity, and good old American pride be made race-neutral and color blind. Is the objective to assert that the rainbow of American humanity has sprung, in full blown illegitimacy, from the forehead of a blindfolded Statue of Liberty? Please. Can any other interpretation be given to a proposal which denies the importance of racial identity?

4. Most racist behavior kicks in when face meets face, regardless of the written record. A conscious elimination of race data will not assure that, in the words of Connerly's *New York Times* profile: ... "He wants to set aside the bulky, contested ledger on America's racial debits and credits," [saying that] "you can't un-ring the bell on slavery. All you can do is make sure the next person who walks through the door, white or black, receives equal treatment."

A more realistic approach, since entry-way bigotry is still alive and well in too much of America, will depend heavily on racial data to verify whether obstructions to equality are real or imagined. Perception may be an individual's reality and hard racial data can confirm or reject patterns of negative perceptions.

5. Reports of a color-blended society, where race does not matter, are premature and greatly exaggerated, at least for African Americans. According to conventional but unrealistic wisdom—and Ward Connerly's *New York Times* profile: "In 10 to 15 years, intermarriage will make this debate a moot one, anyhow, and we'll wonder why we didn't see it coming." Yet, data on race collected by the Federal government do not support this pipe dream.

While the 2000 Census Reports indicate an increased rate of racial intermarriage, a more precise interpretation of these data than Connerly offers paints a more skewed picture. Data confirm that 50 percent of Asians marry non-Asians, usually whites; and that 35–45 percent of Latinos marry non-Latinos, usually whites. However, this same data source confirms that only 4–6 percent of blacks marry non-blacks of any other race.

The myth of the browning of America is grossly distorted, especially for those living in the large metropolitan areas, where visible interracial intimacy exists to a far greater degree than abroad in the land. In fact, the incidence of balkanization, of all-black from all non-black communities, is phenomenal. Analysis of racial data from recent national sample surveys documents that significantly more communities exist today than was the case twenty-five years ago when whites almost never saw a black person in the flesh. Most of these isolated white communities are in the American heartland. One can only conclude, therefore, that it will continue to be unlikely for white-black interracial relationships throughout America to blossom into marriage if there are no black people—and often no other people of color—around. So much for race going out of style and everyone becoming brown pretty soon

6. *There is nothing wrong with helping tax payer-supported institutions to look like America.* As the *Washington Post*/Henry J. Kaiser Family Foundation /Harvard University poll documented last year, gross misperceptions cloud whites views of blacks, on every important measure, including: societal gains, inequitable pay levels, seriousness

of black claims of unfair treatment and access to high-level jobs. For example, four CEO-level blacks among America's 500 top national corporations (Kenneth Chenault at American Express, Richard Parsons at AOL Time Warner, Franklin Raines at Fannie Mae, Stanley O'Neal at Merrill Lynch) do not a ground-swell make. It is these misperceptions in defiance of obvious evidence and commonsense—even when hard racial data is available—that reinforce racial balkanization. Without racial data, things can only get worse.

It is hyperbolic for anyone to claim, as the Racial Privacy Initiative supporters allege, that racial data forces people into jobs and institutions in which they otherwise would not be interested, simply to satisfy artificial racial quotas. Because we have access to data about race, civil rights advocates and well-intentioned public officials have been able to identify career opportunities about which minorities are unaware because a whites-only tradition has been the standard for access. Analysis and documentation of racial data in turn has resulted in the opening of possibilities to previously excluded people of color who then enhance our national resources, our GNP and our global competitiveness.

Especially for most African Americans and many other people of color, race is a visible and palpable reality of daily existence. Until that changes significantly, race must continue to be valued and evaluated. No one, and no decent public policy, should be permitted to make race a shameful, shamed and suppressed human characteristic.

Black and Latina Women Locked in the Jailhouse and the Poorhouse

When fathers, sons, brothers, and other potential family providers are locked in the jailhouse, the women and children in their lives are locked in the poorhouse.

When my late mother, Geneva B. Scruggs, joined her much younger friend, Constance B. Eve, in 1980 to form a volunteer group called Women for Human Rights and Dignity, their selfless goal was to help black women inmates maintain a sense of dignity and family while they did their prison time. The group bought or collected Christmas toys and distributed them to the children of 156 mothers incarcerated in prisons and jails in and around Buffalo, New York.

The volunteers called their holiday effort "Project Joy" because the brightly wrapped Christmas toys and modest personal grooming gifts given to the mothers permitted inmate mothers to save face with their children and maintain their own dignity.

My mother and Connie Eve financed this effort mostly from contributions, which often arrived anonymously at their homes in plain, hand-addressed, white envelopes containing single dollar bills. These tiny donations were made out of deep concern for a disturbing trend toward an ever-growing female prison population that was just beginning to be noticed.

My mother would have been outraged by the deterioration of conditions and the increasing number of black women behind bars since then.

Since Women for Human Rights and Dignity started in 1980, the national women's prison population has grown exponentially, increasing over 500 percent by 1999. The number of female inmates in federal and state correctional facilities was about 13,400 in 1980; in 1998, it had risen to more than 84,400 according to a 1999 United States General Accounting Office Report. Other sources report that the number of female state prisoners convicted of drug-related offenses has increased by 888 percent (almost nine times) from 1986 to 1996.

Draconian criminal justice policies are largely responsible for this accelerated and intensified growth. For example, mandatory sentencing forces judges to issue harsh sentences, particularly in drug-related cases, without regard for otherwise mitigating circumstances, such as first offenses or single motherhood. In 1997, two-thirds of women prisoners had at least one minor child. This policy has been especially harmful to African American and Latina women, who constitute 67 percent of federal and 64 percent of state inmate populations. These women inmates tend to be single parents, either unemployed or with inadequate, low-paying jobs. Given the punitive provisions of welfare reform, they face a lifetime ban in twenty-four states from ever receiving welfare because of their felony convictions.

The Sentences are Inequitable for Black and White Defendants in Cocaine Cases

Sentencing disparities are an equally inequitable consequence of mandatory sentencing, because it requires increased sentences for crack cocaine violations, while offering flexible alternatives in cases arising from powder cocaine arrests. (Powder cocaine is used by predominantly white, middle-class, suburban defendants.)

More than 71 percent of women in federal prison and 35 percent of female state inmates have been convicted of drug offenses, usually involving crack cocaine, which carries mandatory sentences as long as twenty-five years for first time offenders. Moreover, large numbers of women of color convicted of crack offenses have been charged because of relationships with boyfriends, husbands, or other male relatives who themselves are statistically more vulnerable to police apprehension and racial profiling.

Two cases exemplify the numerous other instances of young African American women doing hard time for minor drug involvement.

Kemba Smith, a first-time offender in Virginia, was unable to bargain with prosecutors because she could offer no information about the drug dealer with whom she was romantically involved. She was sentenced to twenty-four years in federal prison (a year in prison for each of her twenty-four years of age) without the possibility of parole.

Many believe, Dorothy Gaines, a mother of two minor children and guardian of two grandchildren, was convicted and is serving a nineteen years, seven months federal sentence without possibility of parole because she had no information to offer against her live-in male companion.

The prison industry, driven by the momentum of privatized prison construction as an effective rural economic development tool, has become self perpetuating. It encourages more convictions, larger prison populations, and longer prison sentences, even though these prisons increasingly have become warehouses for the mothers of black and brown children. In 1995, over $5.1 billion was allocated for new prison construction by federal and state governments, at an average cost of $58,000.00 for a medium security cell. Additional incarceration costs for each inmate exceed $30,000.00 annually, an attractive but diabolical income stream for the prison industry.

Incarceration of Minority Men Puts Minority Women in the Poorhouse

African American and Latina women shoulder another oppressive weight of the criminal justice system. When fathers, sons, brothers, and other potential family providers are locked in the jailhouse, the women and children in their lives are locked in the poorhouse. The Bureau of Justice Statistics and The Sentencing Project Report that late last year nearly one-third of the six million Americans in prison, on probation, or parole (the "3 Ps" of the criminal justice system) were African American males between twenty and twenty-nine. This is the prime age for marriage, initiating fatherhood, and building family economic stability. Instead, the women in these men's lives are alone; serving as single parents and grandparents, raising bail money, carrying the burden of family expenses, defending children and grandchildren against assorted predators, and generally reinforcing the pejorative black-woman-as-head-of-household stereotype.

The profound impact on women of unfair, racially biased law enforcement and criminal justice practices is misunderstood by many, often including male leaders in communities of color. For example, a national press conference was called in 1999 to deplore the targeted destructive effect on communities of color, of biased, unfair, and inequitable treatment of African American and Hispanic men by police and criminal justice system policies and practices. But this otherwise admirable event failed to include a single African American or Hispanic woman leader as a presenter. The total group consisted of thirty-two African American, Hispanic, and white ministers and rabbis—all men—who spoke to a national television and print audience.

Too many black women are being locked in the jailhouse, the

poorhouse, and locked out of the substantive search for viable remedies. No amount of volunteer effort alone can fix that—not even as effective an effort as the 1980 Scruggs-Eve Women for Human Rights and Dignity Initiative that Constance Eve expanded and has successfully continued for decades.

For Black Women: "Life Ain't Been No Crystal Stair"

Black women have been left behind white men and women as well as behind black men on many indicators of American success, including economic and wage parity.

If anyone ought to heed the questionable but compelling command of Chicago's late, powerful and perennial Mayor Richard J. Daley, Sr., it is African American women. Mayor Daley said: "Vote early and often." He then proceeded to remain in office for forty-five years until he died, overwhelming many challenges and difficulties through his political prowess and raw power.

In this year of the first national election in the twenty-first century, many difficulties challenge African American women and their families. Economic and civil rights gains are threatened by intense attacks on affirmative action policies. Programs and resources that support family stability, educational competitiveness, and entrepreneurial opportunities will wax or wane depending upon the outcomes of national as well as local elections. Quality, accessible, and affordable health care is increasingly elusive, especially for single parents and the elderly groups in which black women predominate because a Health Care Bill of Rights is also elusive, hiding in the deep pockets of the health care industry's vested interests.

All of the following have provided a rich resource of concerns challenging black women, many of whom are the primary power centers of their families: Entrepreneur Dr. Jeffalyn Johnson and I conducted a survey of 450 "Black Women in the Middle"; the Joint Center for Political and Economic Studies, a prestigious research institution specializing in African American policy issues has regularly conducted national polls over the past thirty years; and the Black Leadership Forum and the National Political Congress of Black Women have conducted a series of focus during the last four years. The concerns they have identified are:

- Health of the family, a top priority for 64.5 percent of surveyed black women;
- reducing crime and violence within and against black communities, including effective gun control, and family safety and security, cited by 72.4 percent, 40 percent, and 49 percent, respectively, of the respondents and by all focus group participants;
- education of the children, including post-high school and college opportunities, identified by 56.6 percent of such women; and
- "Meeting day-to-day expenses," was cited by one third of all respondents.

The statistics describing black women's conditions translate into a number of incisive questions that should be asked of all political candidates at all levels—federal, state, and local. In the circular system of politics, elected officials not only are responsible for the votes that they cast directly, but also must be held accountable for votes cast by other politicians——at all levels—to whom they give their political fealty and collegial support. Thus, it is important, for example, to hold all Republican senators responsible for the bad behavior of North Carolina Senator Jesse Helms and the Senate Judiciary Committee majority, whose racial animus perpetuates the shame of an historically segregated Fourth Circuit Federal Court of Appeals. Never has an African American jurist gained senate confirmation for appointment to the Fourth Circuit, although 35 percent of all deep south blacks live in the area served by that circuit and 22 percent of the population of that circuit is African American. A vote for a silent, indifferent, or uninformed senator anywhere in the United States is a vote for continued segregation on the Federal Fourth Circuit.

Candidates should be asked where they stand on mandatory sentencing, which disproportionately penalizes African Americans, especially black women whose incarceration rate since 1980 has increased at nearly double the rate for men. Illegal drug possession, arguably the refuge of mentally ill, oppressed, and abused low-income women, accounts for half of this increase. Mandatory sentencing for drug abuse offers no flexibility to women who are first-time offenders or single parents, and who are largely black and Hispanic.

Explicit disclosure should be required of candidates regarding their understanding of and position on state and local policies that encourage Driving-While-Black (DWB) law enforcement excesses. Black women's sons, husbands, brothers, other male relatives, and in fact black women themselves are victims of this racially driven abuse. Families are disrupted and often destroyed by the trauma of DWB-related police brutality and its concomitant jail and/or hospital internments.

Gun control has emerged as a top priority for all women, as was demonstrated by the themes of the Million Mom March this past spring. In the view of African American women, Columbine and other senseless and violent tragedies have brought whites belatedly to a realization long suffered by urban blacks. Guns kill people—wantonly, indiscriminately, often anonymously, always permanently. Candidates who oppose sane gun control laws do not support the family priorities of African American women. A national anti-hand gun policy would be ideal, but state and local legislators also are policy makers on this issue. Probes of all candidates on gun control policies should be followed by election-day penalties and rewards appropriate to the candidates' positions.

Black women have been left behind white men and women, as well as behind black men on many indicators of American success, including economic and wage parity. While women in general earn 72 percent of men's salaries, even after excelling in work experience, education, and merit black women earn even less (60 percent). According to recent analyses by the Lawyers Committee for Civil Rights: "White females and black males must work about eight months to earn a salary equal to what white males earn in six months, [and] black females must work ten months to earn a comparable salary."

Even if voting often is not a legal option, voting early, and in large numbers, is both an option and an imperative for all African Americans, especially women. So, vote for national and local candidates who will appointment more black women with real decision-making authority to critical resource-allocation positions, not just as figure-heads who are not in the decision-making loop. One example of an important power appointment is to the local Workforce Investment Boards, which are the principle vehicles for distributing Federal Department of Labor funds to support job training, essential for Welfare-To-Work efforts. State and local officials, not the Feds, make these important local appointments, which also impact micro-enterprise initiatives. These decisions, in turn, affect the availability of local jobs, especially in the African American community where many single parents are still left behind. For welfare-dependent women, it is local public and private sector employers who determine whether work experiences will be solid career ladder opportunities or dead end trips consisting of simultaneous and serial slave-labor gigs.

Black Women are a Potent, Undervalued, Pivotal Power, Historically Capable of Leveraging in the Interest of Their Own Issues and Priorities

In both the 1992 and 1996 presidential elections, African American women were the voters who provided the margin of victory for President Clinton. Much of the mainstream media perpetuate the myth that a generic "women's vote," apparently meaning all voting women, made the difference in both of these elections. As recently as March 2000, the headline of a *New York Times* article read: "Presidential Race Could Turn on Bush's Appeal to Women," emphasizing presidential candidate Bush's "strong showing among women compared with recent Republican nominees." But these generalities mask a significantly different story and actually ignore the black women's vote.

In 1992 and 1996, exit pollsters reported that white women's votes for Bill Clinton were almost identical to those of white men: 34 percent of white men and 44 percent of white women in 1992; 31 percent of white men and 42 percent of white women in 1996—hardly a winning majority either time, and certainly not a mandate. However, when the African American women's vote was averaged in with the white women's vote, President Clinton was a clear victor. In 1992, 86 percent of black women voted for Clinton, and in 1996, 89 percent voted for the President, raising the "women's" vote to the winning majorities of 54 percent and 51 percent, for those two respective years. Thus, in both elections, white men, white women, and black men (1992: 77 percent and 1996: percent) voted less enthusiastically for Clinton than did black women. Given the ideological and personal distinctions between candidates and their party platforms with regard to African American core issues in the 2000 campaign, black women's stealth power could strike again—if black women turn out to vote.

Confronted by today's polarizing challenges, it is in our own best interest to review meticulously every candidate's record for inconsistencies between our issues and their rhetoric, and then to vote for the candidates whose records' track black women's top priorities. Black women's priorities are life-altering, and survival-driven, because life, for most black women, "ain't been no crystal stair," as African American poet Langston Hughes has poignantly written:

> Life for me ain't been no crystal stair. It's had tacks in it, and splinters and boards torn up, and places with no carpet on the floor, bare. But all the time (I've) been a'climbin on, and reachin' landin's, and turning corners, and sometimes goin' in the dark. Where there ain't been no light....
> ...And life for me ain't been no crystal stair.
>
> (Langston Hughes, "Mother to Son")

The appropriateness of all candidates' remedies for these concerns can be best gauged by their records, not by their rhetoric. Especially in the cases of the Vice President Gore, Senator Liebermann, Governor Bush, and former Senator Richard Cheney, their records are public, specific, accessible, and graphic. Black women, for whom "life ain't been no crystal stair" must carefully examine these records and must not be romanced by rhetoric from cynical minstrels that are more show than substance and that exaggerate the actual participation of black women in the decision-making process within their organizations. Then black women must exercise the majesty of their pivotal power, and vote in November—early, and in great numbers.

Keeping Black Women's Advancements in Perspective

African American women move mountains, literally and figuratively.

In honor of Women's History Month, March's issue of *Ebony*, the sixty-one-year-old monthly magazine from Johnson Publishing Company, is dedicated to black women. For many years, *Ebony* was one of very few national magazines to regularly celebrate African Americans' social, intellectual and political achievements. Even though, in 1960, Dr. Carter G. Woodson's Center for the Study of Negro Life and History set aside the month of February for special tributes to African Americans, if you read *Ebony* every month was "Black History Month." This, of course, is very good for black self-esteem in a world where black accomplishment is ignored by mainstream America. With the rise of feminism women of all colors borrowed that concept from blacks and now also polish their self-esteem every March.

Ebony's March front cover proclaims it the "Annual Women's Issue," making this issue a "two-for" for blacks interested in history (or her-story). The articles inside are a paean to African American women's remarkable accomplishments, only recently publicly recognized in such large numbers. One would think that the black community must be on its way to solid middle-class Nirvana, given the impressive number of black women who have overcome historic obstacles as profoundly suppressed minorities struggling up the success ladder. More than 100 black women are congratulated for their top-ranked jobs in business, industry, Congress, and state and local governments, as well as for their achievements in the more traditional entertainment, sports, and lively arts arenas.

In part, the women featured give an accurate impression of changing fortunes for black women in positions of power in the corporate world. There are new faces in high places these days, quite a few belonging to black women, and none of them are so-called "overnight sensations." Black women have been in the business and industrial arena in large numbers in the past. In fact, recently released "Women's Voices" data, from research by the Center for Policy Alternatives, revealed:

> Women's entrepreneurial spirit remains strong. 40 percent (of the 1200 women surveyed) already own or would like to own their own businesses. Interest is strongest among African American women (39 percent)....

However, this and other studies still confirm that while black women are advancing, there remains a significant income gap for the majority of black women whose average annual earnings are lower than those of black men, white men, and white women.

African American women usually have fully paid their dues and have climbed progressively up the demanding rungs of career ladders, often within the same corporation or institution. Yet, with increasing frequency, they are moving inexorably upward by accepting lateral outside assignments as well. Their profile has been low, or invisible, and their moves discreet, both by choice and by tradition. In that respect, they often have mirrored the traditional profiles of African American women, even during the equal opportunity abuses and systematic violence of the civil rights struggle beginning in the late 1950s. Dr. Britta Nelson, a former research fellow at the Joint Center for Political and Economic Studies and author of *From Protest to Politics: Black Women in the Civil Rights Movement and in the United States Congress* (1998), writes:

> Throughout the 1960s, (Congresswoman Eleanor Holmes) Norton and many other young black women who were involved in the black freedom struggle also developed a high sensibility for gender discrimination. The civil rights movement itself, especially the Student Nonviolent Coordinating Committee (SNCC), which had more women in leadership positions than any other civil rights organization, served as an important catalyst for the new feminism and the Women's Liberation Movement that emerged at that time. ...In their professional lives, especially within the political system, many of the African American women encountered sexism.

I have observed, for example, that every photo of the historic civil rights marches, demonstrations and rallies of the 1960s shows clear images of Dr. Dorothy I. Height, President, National Council of Negro Women; Dr. C. DeLores Tucker, President, National Political Caucus of Black Women; Mrs. Coretta Scott King, President-Emerita, Martin Luther King, Jr. Center for Non-Violent Social Change, and several other unnamed women. They were photographed marching and standing right beside Dr. Martin Luther King, Jr., the Urban League's Whitney Young, the NAACP's Roy Wilkins, and CORE's James Farmer. But national media did then, and still do, refer to the "Big Four" of the civil rights movement, ignoring the ubiquitous black women leaders. In fact, the original leadership decision group, the United Civil Rights Leadership, already meeting monthly by 1963, included *six* (not four) civil rights giants: Dr. King, Roy Wilkins, Whitney Young, James Farmer, and A. Philip Randolph of the Black Activist Union Institute named for him, and Dr. Dorothy Irene Height!

At the sub-national level, even more black women were civil rights leaders, often being the prime strategists for local struggles: Gloria Richardson, an embattled desegregationist from Cambridge, Maryland;

Diane Nash, a steel-nerved, Northern organizer of SNCC in Mississippi; New York attorney Constance Baker Motley, whose lawsuits desegregated public transportation in Jackson, Mississippi; the late Daisy L. Bates, organizer and nurturer of the famous nine Little Rock students who brought down school segregation in Arkansas; and, of course, Fannie Lou Hamer, the pulse of the Mississippi Freedom Democratic Party, who changed the very nature of national democratic nominating conventions. Hamer gets mentioned, lauded, and acknowledged more often than any of the other women civil rights leaders, perhaps because the threat of her power is frozen in history (she died in 1977). Most of the rest live on, although often in obscurity, including Bates, who died in 1999.

Today, African American women have emerged from that tradition of strong leadership to head major subsidiaries of Fortune 500 companies. Some black women whose powerful contributions have not been trivialized are Deborah Steward Coleman (President/CEO AutoAlliance International, owned by Ford Motor Company); Paula A. Sneed (President of the e-commerce and communications divisions of Kraft Foods); Marie C. Johns (President of Verizon, Washington, D.C.); Brenda J. Gaines (President, Citicorp Diners Club North America); Gabriella E. Morris (President, Prudential Foundation); Stacey H. Davis (President, Fannie Mae Foundation); Maxine B. Baker (President/CEO, Freddie Mac Foundation); Ingrid Saunders Jones (Chairwoman, The Coca-Cola Foundation); Pamela Thomas-Graham (President/CEO, CNBC); and, Dr. Bonnie Guiton-Hill (President, Times Mirror Foundation), to name just a few. These are African American women whose decisions can move mountains, with the same determination and job preparation that has already included literal and figurative mountain-moving.

As Dr. Dorothy I. Height always says: "Black women know how to get it done."

Part Two

Media Essays

Imus's Demise Must Herald New Standards

Imus fired a historically market-tested bullet of derogation at every mother, daughter, sister, wife, female relative, partner and/or friend of every woman.

Don Imus has been run over by a fast moving train of his own design. But the engine of that train was the outrage of the many Americans—especially African Americans and women—who know race and gender bashing when they hear it.

When morning news radio and TV mogul Don Imus gratuitously attacked the young women scholar-athletes on Rutgers University's Scarlet Tigers basketball team by calling them disgusting names, he fired a historically market-tested bullet of derogation, not just at those talented physical and intellectual champions. Every mother, daughter, sister, wife, female relative, partner and/or friend of every woman of any color, shared those crosshairs of denigration.

The litany of insults to African American women in particular, and to women in general, is too long, repulsive, and destructive to detail here. These ad homonym attacks repeatedly—from the mouths of Imus, or "gangsta rappers," or some unenlightened entertainers, and/or other racists and sexists—attribute to the low esteem of women and blacks. Public failure to penalize these behaviors simply encourages repetition. It is axiomatic that repetition becomes habit and bad habits become institutionalized. Imus, with all of his warts, reflects the institutional disease of racism, sexism, and the power of notoriety run amuck for everyone to see.

Imus's vitriol disrespected all women. He once again felt the entitlement of his gender, the anonymity of his isolated broadcast studio and the cocoon of intimacy with his snickering white buddies. Like others with high public position, he has repeatedly relieved himself of his deepest basic instincts and called it comedy. This time, the spew of his diatribe has leaped well beyond the established decency barrier.

He now says that he went too far. Since I believe that to be true, it is appropriate for him to be deprived immediately of another turn at bat and thus end the opportunities for him to break this most recent homerun record for racial and gender slander.

Don Imus earned the punishment which MSNBC announced by firing him. This justifiable decision was endorsed not only by CBS also, but by a large number of the sponsors of Imus's media exposure. Their actions herald, I hope, a transition from an anarchy of permissiveness on the airways to a zero tolerance policy toward public media excesses and indecency, at long last.

Better late than never.

This same admonition applies to the justice and equity advocacy community. We still have much work to do in publicly penalizing verbal and other abuses to which African Americans and all women are subjected regularly. More cleaning up of abusive and disrespectful language will not take place without more targeted agitation. The ball is now in our court.

Black Leaders and The Urban Policy Institutes

It is important for local leaders to combine their rich experiences into local strategies for urban change.

There is a window of opportunity for local urban leaders, especially those who represent the black and Latino communities, to advance some of the solutions to urban problems which they have been nurturing for so many years.

It is true that the urban revolt in Los Angeles in May of last year refocused the general public's attention on the crises in our inner-cities. It also is true that as a result of the drama of Los Angeles, many people have been coming forward from many quarters—academic, research and political—to offer remedies to urban problems like those in L.A.

But until L.A. hit the front pages of daily newspapers and was reported on primetime network television, it had been difficult to get most politicians or pundits to pay much attention to the plight of cities. Thus, Los Angeles was a very mixed blessing: it reflected one of the worst possible results of urban neglect; but its re-emphasis on the decline in the quality of urban life provided a welcome opportunity for action.

There is a cadre of seasoned urban leaders who have had responsibility for the city's problems for the last decade. They have continued to provide needed services and assistance, even while their efforts have been under-funded. They have been advocates for those who increasingly have stood outside the mainstream of marketplace benefits. They have patched together a quilt of ad hoc solutions to thorny problems confronting blacks and Latinos, and to some degree, Asians also, in our urban communities.

Their efforts have not had the benefit of a responsive national urban agenda. And, usually, neither time nor resources have allowed for coordination with other similar local efforts, or have afforded the opportunity to learn from the experiences of others or replicate successes already proven elsewhere.

Now is the time for these leaders to share and publicize—at the local and national levels—reports on these individual, local, and national levels—reports on these individual, local accomplishments. It is important for local leaders to combine their rich experiences into local strategies for urban change. The Joint Center for Political and Economic Studies has created a vehicle, The Urban Policy Institutes, to help local leaders in communities across the country in refining and consolidating urban strategies. These leaders speak for the black and Latino communities because they were working there, even when it was not newsworthy to do so. These leaders believe that their insight should guide national policy for their cities, and not vice versa.

The Scientifically Reasoning City

Targeted tandem efforts did an excellent job of renewing the urban environment, as well as rebuilding both communities and self-esteem through various kinds of job and employment training.

Why is it that scientists who investigate physical, biological, or astronautical problems always replicate and constantly refine past solutions, but social scientists who specialize in urban problems regularly ignore past remedies and constantly search for a "new solution"?

In recent conferences and roundtable discussions where experts on cities have exchanged views, there often is caution in not suggesting ideas from The Great Society Era, and, heaven forbid, don't cite The Poverty Program, or old catchphrases like "Model Cities" and "Comprehensive Planning."

I think that we in the urban professions are beginning to believe the propaganda of our critics, who have cavalierly dismissed a twenty-year period of social and urban reform as a failure. I also think that this is fallacious reasoning. Not only were Head Start and The Work Incentive Program for Dependent Mothers very effective, but targeted tandem efforts between the departments of HUD, Labor and Commerce did an excellent job of renewing the urban environment, as well as rebuilding both communities and self-esteem through various kinds of job and employment training.

UDAG, which stood for the now defunct Urban Development Action Grant is not a bad four-letter word. This joint venture between private developers, banks, and local and federal governments stimulated capital investment by all four and produced enduring benefits for many low-income individuals and communities, which continued long after the initial UDAG project was completed.

Citizen participation, for all of the nervousness which it produced in incumbent elected officials, was the best example of democracy-at-work since the town meetings of the eighteenth century. And CETA offered MSNY grassroots folk, especially minorities, an unprecedented ladder out of poverty. It was a useful form of local public service employment.

Cities are at least as important as space stations. We should apply the scientific method to both.

Beyond Shopping Black

Rebuild the black community educationally, economically, culturally and spiritually—go beyond just shopping black.

Recently, the national press reported on an approach to the revitalization of low-income areas, which is being tried successfully in Los Angeles. The approach is called "Buying Black" and its objective is to strengthen the black community, which was pushed over the brink by last year's South Central revolt, after a long, sustained slide down the hill of neglect and indifference. By encouraging black people, regardless of their own residential locations, to invest their dollars in businesses and banks which are located in predominantly black neighborhoods, this strategy responds to the frustration of persistent economic decline in south Los Angeles as well as in many other urban minority neighborhoods.

What is new about the Los Angeles experience is not that "Buying Black" is being tried. What is new, is that the strategy seems to be working. $8.5 million dollars, of the $9.5 billion dollars of liquid assets controlled by blacks in Los Angeles County, has flowed back into the black community, initially through fund transfers by black churches into small, black-owned banks. Other targeting strategies include shopping where blacks are visibly employed and supporting a city-wide program by patronizing black owned establishments which display a "Recycling Black Dollars" sign in their windows.

In 1992, I wrote a report for the Joint Center entitled: "Developing the Black Community." I proposed, as one of four alternative development approaches, the encirclement and rebuilding of the black community by the black community: educationally, economically, culturally and spiritually. This approach goes beyond shopping black. It also extends to: educating young black males; extended community parenting for young children; life-long adult education; and, systematic community fund-raising to underwrite the costs of institutions which assist black residents and families.

The Darkening Diversity

A new American democracy must build bridges of exchange, collaboration, coalition and accommodation.

Sometimes I hear in the ear of my mind the refrain of an old spiritual from my youth in African-American churches: "My Lord, it's so high I can't get over, and it's so wide I can't get 'round it, it's so low I can't get under…. I must cross over and go through the land."

It's a poignant echo and, unfortunately, not just an echo of things past. I most often hear this refrain when I think about the growing balkanization within and between our communities, especially those communities where the people look, more or less, more like me than like Anglo-Saxon America: the Latino, Mexican and Hispanic communities; the Asian communities, whether Korean, Japanese, Chinese, Vietnamese or Pacific, rim the continental African and the Caribbean communities; and of course, the African American community.

With the demographic changes of the last decade, our central cities have become more diverse than ever, and the diversity has become darker than ever before, both literally and figuratively.

Literally, almost 40 percent of America's total population growth during the last decade was from immigration. Of that 40 percent, three-quarters of these immigrants were black, brown and tan: 35 percent Asian and 45 percent Latino/Hispanic. The vast majority of these newest minorities settled in America's ten largest cities. Moreover, these cities of their destination, and other congested, distressed metropolitan areas (mostly concentrated in the Northeast and Midwest except for Los Angeles and

Miami,) are home to three out of four African-Americans.

This distribution has led, also, to the darkening figurative quality of diversity: new, largely poor minority people compete tensely and hostilely with largely poor <u>established</u> minority people for older housing, lower-skilled jobs and shared cultural space—all of which are ever diminishing, in both quality and quantity.

A new American democracy must build bridges of exchange, collaboration, coalition and accommodation. It is for "crossing over" and for "going through the land" that we need human bridges. Black Americans should take the lead. We have had more experience with this land than anyone.

Vessels of Our Collective Future

The scourges in America's inner cities of long term unemployment and the concomitant destruction and violence of a crack-cocaine industry demand that the community once again become the parents of this generation's psychologically and economically orphaned young children.

At the beginning of the settlement house movement, near the start of the twentieth century, neighborhood leaders and their benefactors took personal responsibility for the welfare of children. The community centers, located in churches, served as models for the community centers that the neighborhood settlement houses became. Together, these sectarian and non-sectarian havens fed, clothed, guided, sheltered, inspired, trained, and even educated urban children of the streets.

Many, although not all, of the children who were rescued came from very poor homes, from broken homes, and from drunken, dysfunctional and neglectful parents, who often were themselves victims. Today, conditions for children in urban communities are worse than they were then.

Now, at the end of the twentieth century, a revolution of values and economic conditions in this country is once again permitting the children to fall through the cracks of organized society into the abyss of homelessness, orphanage and general neglect. The scourges in America's inner cities of long term unemployment and the concomitant destruction and violence of a crack-cocaine industry demand that the community once again become the parents of this generation's psychologically and economically orphaned young children.

We must seriously explore the benefits of developing "children's villages," a series of residential shelters and surrogate, alternative group homes located away from these diseased communities. And we must do this in order to "quarantine" our children from the raging urban patterns of drug use and violence. If long-term care and maintenance in "children's villages" is available for these very young vessels of our collective futures, then they will have protective and nurturing environments committed to their very survival as productive, contributing citizens of tomorrow. This is a community responsibility now, just as it was when this century began.

The Race Debate

As long as there is evidence that African Americans are excluded from participation on an equal basis in the benefits of American society, race is important and needs to be discussed.

Princeton philosopher Cornel West writes that "race matters." I agree. I am having great difficulty understanding the apparently increasing conventional wisdom that race-neutrality offers an effective solution to the relationship which exists today between African Americans and white Americans.

I read that candidates for high public office, who happen to be African Americans, are found wanting because they constantly seek to open the dialogue on race and to examine publicly and directly ways in which the "matter of the color line," in the immortal words of the W.E.B. Du Bois, can be eliminated. We are led to believe that the fact of such a discussion in and of itself leads to the reality of racial consciousness, or racism rather than just the other way around, which is my own personal experience.

It seems to me that, as long as I as an African American woman, can fully expect to be confronted by anonymous white Americans, and sometimes also members of other ethnic groups, with stereotypic views of how I should be treated and what I am entitled to, race is important and needs to be discussed. As long as there is evidence that African Americans are excluded from participation on an equal basis in the benefits of American society, race is important and needs to be discussed.

Some others share this view. During the last couple of years a bestselling book re-emphasized that there is a "closing door on black opportunity," according to Gary Orfield. In the book, *Race in America*, he states that racism is on the increase; moreover, the Eisenhower Foundation has just issued a study which reports more racism in America than there was twenty-five years ago, after the Watts uprising. And, Andrew Hacker writes about *Two Nations: Black and White, Separate, Hostile, Unequal.*

Those who would deny a measured dialogue on race undermine American democracy and reject equality.

Hardcore Rap Does Not Deserve A Constitutional Shield

Misogynist assaults whether visual, verbal, or physical are all on the same rape continuum.

When African Americans finally enjoy all of the benefits of the American Constitution with a special emphasis on the unfulfilled promises of the fourteenth and fifteenth Amendments—then and only then—will I begin to appreciate the argument that hardcore rappers and misogynist video performers ought to be afforded First Amendment protections for their foul and denigrating portrayals of black girls and women. It is appalling that any sane, respectable person would seek shelter for the abuse and insult of misogynistic rap lyrics and video images under the guise of Constitutional infringement.

Literally hundreds of thousands of African American youth show incontrovertible evidence of misplaced and lost values and self esteem through their over representation in the ranks of school drop outs; of the unemployed and underemployed; and of participants in the criminal justice system. And whatever blame belongs to the racism and inequality of the American society for these statistics, and believe me, a great deal of the blame belongs exactly there, there also is plenty of blame to assign to African American adults who condone and fail to reject such filthy and derogatory imagery—whether verbal or visual— of the mothers, daughters and sisters of the black community.

The complicity of the media and the entertainment industry (undeniably not controlled by the black community) in the marketing of this misogyny is obvious. Is it then far fetched to conceive of a genocidal outcome from a strategy which so closely parallels practices in warring nations, throughout history as well as today, of destroying a nationality's resolve by assaulting and devaluing the women who are their very genesis? Misogynist assaults whether visual, verbal, or physical are all on the same rape continuum.

Too many black youth are being handsomely rewarded for venting their anger, hate and hostility about their victimizing life experiences through misogyny masquerading as entertainment. In turn, these performers both victimize and blame the other victims in their own embattled communities, black girls and women. African American men and women, in collaboration with responsible American adults of every race must reject misogynist entertainment and unite to fashion alternative avenues to acceptance and respectability for young black males.

Career Photos

58

Career Photo Identification List

Page 56 (L–R):
Dr. John Hope Franklin.

Arlene Holt, Baker, Dr. Dorothy I. Height, YSL (with hat), NLC's Matt Losak, and Professors Linda DeLoach and Elise Bryant

Ambassador Carol Moseley Braun.

John Bryant; Professor Derrick A. Bell, Jr. Esq.

Alexis Herman, 23rd U.S. Secretary of Labor.

(Standing far right) David Rockefeller, YSL, and the major top executives of New York State's housing and economic development establishment.

YSL receiving the Howard University Graduate Research Faculty Award.

Page 57 (T–B, L–R):
YSL's husband, Edward V. Leftwich; Hillary Clinton and President Bill Clinton.

YSL (far left); Mayor James Tate (front center with stripped tie); Joe Oberman (laughing); and the Philadelphia Model Cities staff.

Congressman John Conyers.

Madam Leah Tutu and YSL's daughter, Rebecca.

Page 58 (T–B, L–R):
Verizon's Oscar Gomez; Del Vasquez; YSL and Vernon E. Jordan, Jr., Esq.

Dr. Jewelle Taylor Gibbs; Dr. Mary Frances Berry; Eddie N. Williams.

Percy E. Sutton, Esq.; Honorable Arthur O. Eve.

Alice Walker; Melanie Campbell (center rear,) and YSL (in cap).

YSL being sworn in as Deputy Mayor of Philadelphia, P.A., by the late Judge Julian King; Mayor Wilson Goode is seated (rear); and Philip Hilton holds *Bible*.

Page 59 (L–R):
Honorable Chairman Charles B. Rangel.

Journalist/Author Rev. Dr. Barbara Reynolds.

Dr. Dorothy I. Height.

Coretta Scott King.

Dr. Wangari Maathai (standing next to YSL); Dr. Dorothy I Height (seated); others in photo include Ghanaian Ambassador to the U.S. (standing behind YSL); Vivian Smith, and Vivian Derrick (on far left and far right).

Page 60 (L–R):
Rev. Dr. Joseph E. Lowery; and Rev. Edward V. Leftwich.

White House Press Corps Dean, Journalist Helen Thomas.

Energy Secretary Hazel O'Leary.

William Coleman, Esq.

Page 61 (T–B, L–R):
Dr. Cynthia McCollum and NBC/LEO President E.W. Cromartie.

Secretary Patricia Roberts Harris swearing YSL in as HUD's Deputy Assistant Secretary for Community Planning and Development. YSL's daughters, Cathryn D. Perry and Geneva-Rebecca Scruggs Perry (nearest YSL) holds *Bible*.

Secretary Pat Harris.

The late Jessie Rattley, and the director of their Model Cities Administration at right of YSL.

Congressman Wellington Web.

Page 62 (L–R):
YSL's swearing-in ceremony in home town of Buffalo, N.Y., to the SUNY College–Buffalo Board of Trustees with many family members, including sister Roslyn Scruggs.

YSL with Berlin, Germany graduate school students during her Fulbright Fellowship.

N.Y. Atty. Gen. Bob Abrams; Florence M. Rice; and Dr. Bonnie Guiton Hill.

YSL with Dr. Lowery (Black Leadership Forum event).

YSL and the women of Alpha Chi Chapter, Alpha Kappa Alpha Sorority.

Part Three

Speeches and Public Addresses

Leveraging Our Legacy to Lift Our City

Intellectual aggression and vigor have inspired values of equality and parity.

President Jenkins, students, trustees, faculty and staff of University of the District of Columbia; public officials, members of the clergy, friends: Thank you for your gracious invitation to me, to join with you in this learning community, at this landmark convocation, for an institution which I have known for many, many of its years of evolution and productivity.

I have, in fact, known UDC in various of its permutations and combinations…, longer, even, than I have known your President, my friend, colleague and most worthy adversary—Dr. Timothy Jenkins. This is a sweep of years which shall remain diplomatically unquantified, in the interest of both my and President Jenkins's veil of mystery about our ages…of course, his more than my own.

However, suffice it for me to say that I first knew UDC as the "Federal City College." "Back in that day," as young people now refer to the bygone era, I came to Howard University from the University of Pennsylvania, where I was on faculty and also had just completed my Ph.D. residency, to chair Howard's graduate department and create their undergraduate department for city and regional planning. It was an era when a number of Howard University faculty also taught at Federal City College, and when Federal City students often segued into matriculation at Howard, frequently going back and forth between the two institutions to earn a degree.

When Federal City became the University of the District of Columbia in 1974, there was much of the same sense of liberation and self-determination as there was later for the home rule for the district itself. It was expected that a new era in local higher education had arrived, and that with this advent, would come an intellectual vigor which would be more meshed with the life of Washington's grass roots citizens than was the case with any of the other universities in town. Those of us who were fighting for home rule, identified also with the college of the common person—as we euphemistically viewed UDC to be. It is most gratifying, therefore, for me to celebrate this jubilee opening with you especially since as an academic institution you stand on a precipice of great possibility, in an environment of singular challenge, in a geographic place of profound contradiction. I personally feel quite at home here with you at that convergence of possibility, challenge and contradiction, the very essence of Washington, D.C. I sincerely hope that you also feel at home in this literal and figurative "place."

I recognize, of course, that, for my own part, I am living out a particular love affair with Washington, D.C., which began for me many years ago when I was a young teenager, living in my birthplace in upper New York state. My mother, an educator and early civil rights activist, was using her creativity to help me pursue my then-career goal of becoming a civil rights lawyer. My father had reservations about her strategy which would take me south to a historically black university for my pre-law training rather than my attending college at home in Buffalo, New York. But my mother and I had devised a plan which would provide the money for my HBCU education, including the travel, out-of-state fees and dormitory living. I would enter the then-famous oratorical contest sponsored by the Fraternal Organization International Benevolent Protected Order of Elks of the World, become the winner of the top prize of a scholarship which would take care of the HBCU costs, and be on my way.

The Elks oratorical contest was a natural for me. According to my father, I always possessed a "gift of gab." But the oration, which had to be original and delivered from memory, also had to address an important theme of the day. Now, there are defining moments for most individuals when some experience, some event, some element of predestination decides forever the course of their lives. In many respects, the development of my oration for the Elks oratorical contest, the internalization of its message (as I memorized all ten minutes of its text, not more than ten minutes, not less than ten minutes, ten minutes exactly, according to the oratorical rules,) the living-out of the oration, and finally, the winning of the scholarship, influenced my life forever.

My mother and I chose the theme: our constitutional guarantees of freedoms. And, just as the first lines of some literary classics are inscribed forever in the minds of some people who read them, like: "It was the best of times, it was the worst of times", from Charles Dickens's *A Tale of Two Cities*. Or another favorite classic: "All happy families are alike, but unhappy families are unhappy, each after their own fashion" which is the opening sentence from Tolstoy's classic opus, *Anna Karinina*. So, also, will I never forget the opening lines on my Elks contest oration:

"I went to Washington the other day, and I stood on Capitol Hill. My heart beat fast as I viewed the majestic presence of our federal government. The guarantees of the Constitution of the United States of America, and the power of the Bill of Rights and the full promise of the Declaration of Independence, which found expression in the halls of Congress before me, echoed inside my head: 'We hold these truths to be self-evident, that all men are created equal; that they are endowed by their creator with the inalienable rights, that among these are the rights to life, liberty and the pursuit of happiness' (these were no longer empty phrases, but demands for freedom and justice for all people) 'regardless of race, religion or national origin.'"

Through these words I had fallen in love with Washington, D.C., with the promise which its existence represented for me, with the U.S. Constitution which Washington, D.C. symbolized, and with the notion that this was my country and that Washington, D.C. was the capitol of my nation. In retrospect, this epiphany was made all the more dramatic, at least inside me, by the fact that, not only had I never actually been to Washington, D.C., (although my oration eloquently described the literal and figurative place), but also, I had never been anywhere in or near the South. My parents were afraid that my big mouth and independent attitude would get me, and them, since as a youngster I was unlikely to be traveling alone—strung up on some tree!

But my passionately complex love affair with Washington was the vehicle for my journey inside democracy, not unlike the journey taken by so many whose minds have been the crucible, the breeding ground, of their own destiny and whose intellectual aggression and vigor have inspired values of equality and parity in the service of full democratic citizenship and vision.

The late, distinguished and self-selected Washingtonian, Patricia Roberts Harris, lawyer, educator, ambassador, HUD secretary, health, education and welfare (later Health and Human Services Secretary); spoke of this civic imperative locked in the intellectual community of the academy in a speech which she gave at Harvard University's Kennedy School over twenty years ago. Attorney Pat Harris said:

> The Declaration of Independence and the Constitution define this nation's aspirations and values more completely than twentieth century cynics are willing to acknowledge. ...Conservatives and liberals

will agree that it is indeed the task of government to provide for the general welfare and to expand the blessings of liberty to all citizens. The problems arise, not in the statement of purpose, but in securing agreement on the best way to achieve the purpose. ... Although courageous political leadership will recognize the bankruptcy of the old concepts, it is the intellectual community that must provide the justification for new approaches to the issues of national life.... The plain facts are that the most troubling problems facing society, racism and chronic poverty, for example, will take more than a quick fix or a four year plan to turn around. What we must prepare ourselves for is a much longer and more constant struggle for change.

It is from within the prophesy of these words of Harris's that I wish to cast my comments to you today. It is out of the convergence of possibility, challenge and contradiction which is "Washington, D.C. — manifest," that I wish to revisit the promise of the University of the District of Columbia and the intellectual richness of its human resources—students and faculty. But we come to this dialogue today in shock and in trauma, generated by the breach in our security shield, the corruption of our mental posture of invulnerability, and bewilderment that an armed force of people exists, outside and within our nation, who are capable of converting themselves, personally, into weapons of mass destruction, perhaps to the tenth power and even higher.

In a commentary which I wrote recently, which will run tomorrow in the *Chicago Tribune* newspaper, I challenged us all to connect the dots and understand the causal links between the World Conference Against Racism, Racial Discrimination, Xenophobia and Related Intolerance, just concluded on September 8, 2001, in Durban, South Africa, and the dastardly September 11, terrorist attack against the United States of

America. Coming on the heels of Durban's stressful confrontation between nations ideologically, and also often geographically polarized, and following in the wake of rending and tendentious displays of the industrialized nations', particularly the United States, raw power in thwarting a race conference agenda which addressed long-neglected third world issues, the specter of the deadly imploding concrete and steel of America's economic and military superiority was unfathomable.

The acts of human annihilation, perpetrated by U.S. airplanes which were turned into situational weapons of mass destruction in the hands of lunatics, instantly trivialized the conference's posturing, bickering and frequent fits of uncompromising arrogance. The image of discord projected by many who reported on the World Conference Against Racism (WCAR) was fueled by western nations' determination to have their own way and to play only by their own rules. As long as petty parliamentary moves succeeded in suppressing slavery and reparations as topics for serious consideration, western power ruled. As long as it was possible for extremists on all sides—Arabs, Israelis and Americans—to manipulate the Middle East into an untenable zero-sum position, no nation could be required to make true progress on slavery, its lingering effects or its remedies. Yet, these heated confrontations somehow pale when compared with the United States' utter vulnerability under a war-like attack, or with the fragility of thousands of Americans' lives, collaterally consumed in a conflagration of hatred and fanatical rage.

But, the dots do somehow connect in my mind. There appears, in shifting images and recollections, to be a link between the negotiating, collaborating, rapprochement-seeking delegates at WCAR—the majority of whom seemed to be women, from both the industrialized West and also from the third world—and the allegedly "third world"

71

kamikaze men who, in a matter of moments, shook the foundations—literally, spiritually and figuratively—of America's deeply embedded sense of security. We here in Washington still stagger from the realization that our complacency was great enough for the icon of world military preparedness, the pentagon, to consequently lie in rubble just across the Fourteenth Street bridge.

My WCAR experience was that it was the international team of women who planned, governed, managed, guided, mediated and finally led the fragile World Conference Against Racism, complete with a minimally acceptable formal conference declaration and a plan of action to a conclusion. This experience suggests that we will need increasingly more such open-minded people at the boundaries between the U.S., our sworn enemies and the rest of the world if, in the months to come, we are to prosecute with any sanity a campaign against specifically identified groups of terrorists and their networks, to avenge the pain and destruction caused by the now infamous attack.

WCAR would not have gotten beyond the first preparatory conference had it not been for the tenacity of UN High Commissioner/Secretary General of WCAR, Mary Robinson, who repeatedly insisted that racism is a legitimate topic for discussion and that a nation's failure to show up is a part of the problem, and not a responsible solution. This message was lost on the U.S. which now must seek alliance with some of the same governments which did consider racism to be important and, in spite of differences and disclaimers, hung in until the exhausting end. Others joined with High Commissioner Robinson, hoping to keep the U.S. at the table and also to soothe the irritated feelings of international representatives, governmental as well as non-governmental, who considered America's attitude insulting and dismissive. Women like Barbara Arnwine, Esq., chair of the Drafting Committee, Adjoa

Aiyetoro, Esq., co-chair of the African-African Descendants Caucus, both Americans, and South Africa's Minister for Foreign Affairs Dr. Nkosazana Dlamini Zuma, were a few of these others.

Yet, it will be from among many of the third world nations that the U.S. will seek allies, collaborators, coalition partners—and advice—as our government's top leaders try to move a retaliation agenda forward and to reconfigure our strategy for assuring the U.S. first strike preeminence. My country, and it is, indeed, my country, built and paid for with the very essence of my ancestors, has engendered bad feelings across the globe. A Blue Ribbon Commission co-chaired by former Senator Gary Hart and former Congressman Newt Gingrich recently reported that America is viewed by a majority in the world as having a bad attitude. In addition to being ejected from the U.N. Commission on Human Rights, the U.S. reneged on the Kyoto Protocol, intended to control and manage global warming, and received a very negative review of its six-year-overdue report to the U.N. Committee on the elimination of racial discrimination. We are going to have a hard time building anti-terrorism alliances with a number of countries affected by this behavior.

The distinguished African American philosopher, Alain Leroy Locke, long neglected but by the most diligent scholars of racism and race relations in the world as well as in the United States, wrote definitively about the importance of "race" as a viable construct in civilization. At the turn of the last century, in the early 1900s, Professor Locke argued that races, as products of culture, were constantly undergoing change. Rather than viewing blacks and whites as extremely different types as W.E. B. Du Bois had done, Locke saw blacks and whites as highly assimilative beings: blacks had assimilated Anglo-American culture to a large degree, just as whites had imbibed African American culture. In this regard, the discussion about race was a tri-partite one, involving as it did not only the definitional tensions between Du Bois and Locke, but including as well the concepts of Franz Boas, the father of American anthropology, whose early studies of racial traits and whose pioneer volume, *The Mind of The Primitive Man*, revolutionized theories of race and culture.

Boas believed that the solution to the racial problem required that we de-emphasize race in modern life and assimilate ethnic groups totally into the dominant American stock. But Locke wished to retain the concept of race. He did not accept the proposition that race was either a permanent biological entity or nothing at all. ...Locke recognized that for peoples of color in the twentieth century, the issue of race was linked to the reality of modern imperialism and saw how that imperialism affected their lives and cultures.

In his 1920s treatise on racial progress and race adjustment, Professor Locke wrote:

> Race as a unit of social thought is of permanent significance and of growing importance. It is not to be superseded except by some revised version of itself. Too much social thinking has gone into it for it to be abandoned as a center of thought or of practice. To redeem, to rescue or to revise that thought and practice should be the aim of race theorists and those who want to educate people into better channels of group living.

An extension of the contemporary American viewpoint that we all should just "get over all of this race talk" and, in the sentiments of a battered Rodney King, "...just get along" was the decision of the United States to pass up the opportunity to share such a rich, deep and intellectually stimulating dialogue. What a waste of minds and spirits and a history of growing through adversity, as African Americans and other United States people of color have done, by our government's shallow understanding of American diversity.

Well, I believe that the connection between the WCAR, that raucous global gathering of people arguing about ways to eliminate racism, which the U.S. rejected out of hand, and the cross-hairs of pure terror in which we Americans today perceive ourselves to be, is more linear than not. The dots connect. We need allies, but unless we exhibit greater finesse and class in joining in the debate as part of the solution rather than as the problem, we are going to have one devil of a time in attracting them.

One of my important mentors, the late Judge A. Leon Higginbotham, wrote in his most searching book, *Shades of Freedom*, about Justice Thurgood Marshall's speech given just six months before he died, outlining his vision for America:

> I wish I could say that racism and prejudice were only distant memories... And that liberty and equality were just around the bend. I wish I could say that America has come to appreciate diversity and to see and accept similarity. But as I look around, I see not a nation of unity but of division, afro and white, indigenous and immigrant, rich and poor, educated and illiterate.... But there is a price to be paid for division and isolation.

> We cannot play ostrich. Democracy cannot flourish amid fear. Liberty cannot bloom amid hate. Justice cannot take root amid rage. We must go against the prevailing wind. We must dissent from the indifference. We must dissent from the apathy. We must dissent from the fear, the hatred and the mistrust. We must dissent from a government that has

left its young without jobs, education or hope. We must dissent from the poverty of vision and the absence of moral leadership. We must dissent because America can do better, because America has no choice but to do better. Take a chance won't you? Knock down the fences that divide. Tear apart the walls that imprison. Reach out; freedom lies just on the other side.

But, what should you do...what should each of us do.... To draw on the robust history of this University of the District of Columbia's learning community, and upon the strong intellectual tradition which Pat Harris felt to be at the core of America's successful innovative governance and resolute definition of national purpose? Is it enough simply to identify the dilemma and then to curse the darkness? Or is it all of our intellectually responsible assignments to light the candles?

Based upon my life and my experience, upon my steadfast determination to reject any attempt to deprive me of my American birthright, upon my persistent tilting at windmills with the tools of research and analysis most firmly in my own possession, based upon all of this evidence of "things seen and unseen," in the eloquent words of James Baldwin, I think that those of us gathered here today have an obligation to be active parts of the solution. I often tell my students, who mostly study political power and urban planning constructs, that clients need very little help in forming protests and voicing their dissatisfaction with status quo conditions—they can do that on their own—what they really need is measured, substantive, documented strategies, preferably in written form, for designing and implementing solutions.

The District of Columbia is a worst case example of the failure of the Constitution of the United States to protect all Americans. But the

Constitution designed three branches of government, and without strong political allies in places other than Washington, the probability of the Congressional Branch's approval of statehood for D.C. is remote. It is not necessarily anything other than the protection of the balance of political power which creates the obstacle. The solution lies beyond D.C.'s borders. Analyses are needed to design and implement a specific national strategy for gaining D.C.'s statehood.

I shall close with two thoughts, each from people who have been where you are and who care about the continuing quality of your institution:

In *The Fire Next Time*, James Baldwin writes:

> Everything now, we must assume, is in our hands: we have no right to assume otherwise. If we—and now I mean the relatively conscious whites and the relatively conscious blacks (and other people of color) who must, like lovers, insist on, or create, the consciousness of the others—do not falter in our duty now, we may be able, handful that we are, to end the racial nightmare, and achieve our country, and change the history of the world. If we do not now dare everything, the fulfillment of that prophecy, recreated from the bible in song by a slave, is upon us. God gave Noah the rainbow sign, no more water, the fire next time.

But Mrs. Mary McLeod Bethune, founder of the National Council of Negro Women, world-class presidential advisor and sage beyond all others, left a gentler mandate—one which guided, in all probability, the women who mediated the World Conference Against Racism a couple of weeks ago. Mrs. Bethune's message was:

> I leave you love. Love builds. It is positive and helpful. It is more

beneficial than hate. Injuries are quickly forgotten, quickly pass away. Personally and racially our enemies must be forgiven. Our aim must be to create a world of fellowship and justice, where no man's skin color, or religion, is held against him. "Love thy neighbor" is a precept which could transform the world if it were universally practiced. It connotes brotherhood (and sisterhood) and, to me, brotherhood (and sisterhood are) the noblest concepts in all human relations. Loving your neighbor means being interracial, interreligious and international.

These credos are the same, but also, they are polar opposites. For me, my truth lies somewhere in between, from Robert Frost:

> For the woods are lovely, dark and deep, but I have promises to keep, and miles to go before I sleep, and miles to go before I sleep.
> (Robert Frost, "Stopping by Woods on a Snowy Evening")

Always Look a Gift Horse in the Mouth: Things are Not Always as They Seem

Cultures depend upon institutions and traditions for the perpetuation of their values and strengths.

Good friends, with whom we have shared rich life experiences, are never more than a thought away from resuming the threads of that relationship; thus, it is with your Vice President and my friend, the honorable Public Official and Attorney, Dr. Shirley M. Dennis. Thinking of her, and fondly recalling the drama of our not-too-distant, common pasts, instantly reminds me of an equally gracious poem by that early nineteenth century poet, Lord Byron:

> She walks in beauty, like the night
> Of cloudless climes and starry skies;
> And all that's best of dark and bright
> Meet in her aspect and her eyes:
> Thus mellowed to that tender light
> Which heaven to gaudy day denies.
>
> (Lord Byron, "She Walks in Beauty")

Thank you, my friend, for your warm and gracious introduction.

Good morning, degree candidates of the first Cheney University graduating class of the twenty-first century.

Congratulate your selves, again and again, Dr. Pettus; commencement ceremony participants; parents of the graduates, and other relatives; members of the board of trustees and other university family members;, and my own family, Professor Sally A. Ross, who was once a part of your university family, and who is kind to accompany me here today; and other university faculty, colleagues and friends. Good morning and happy commencement to you all.

Being invited to speak at your commencement is, for me, an invitation to return to that idyllic period in my own development when I explored my own possibilities. When I searched for new avenues to freedoms not yet experienced. When I probed limits not yet tested. The mandatory punches on the union card had been made. The requirements of parents, of legacy, of basic academic expectations had been met, at least minimally, by the prevailing standards of that time, which, to some extent still apply today in this time. I was graduating into full adulthood and, simultaneously, I was "commencing" upon a journey, of my life and my life's work.

At that age, just on the far side of the teen years, there seemed to be little difference between "my life" and Amy work," at least as I projected these images in my active and dramatic imagination. I was then, had always been, and remain to this day, an activist and an advocate for change. And so, my tenure as president of Women's Student Government Assembly and as Editor-in-Chief of the award-winning student newspaper, at the public "HBCU" then called North Carolina College and now known as North Carolina Central University, made me confident that I had gathered the tools, the tenacity and the temerity to change things through active advocacy.

I even believed that I could eventually overcome the disappointing lessons learned as the first woman ever to compete for election to the presidency of our school-wide student government. And the first also to lose that contest because, as my neighbors in the all women's dormitory for junior class women told me, "...a man ought to be president of student government, not a woman." Unfortunately, I had not yet heard the admonitions of The Serenity Prayer:

Lord, give me the serenity to accept the things I cannot change, the courage to change the things that I can, and the wisdom to know the difference.

As I visit with you today, then, I reflect on how my life has played itself out, and upon what lessons I learned which still have validity, which I might safely pass on to you and what instructions best fit your circumstances and your milieu and can be adapted to the unique demands of this new century. There are still some things which need repeating, which we need to keep doing until we all get it right. But, I also draw for that assignment, upon recommendations from other sources whom I have specifically polled on your behalf, to offer advice and guidance especially intended for you, the Cheney State University bachelor's and master's degree candidates of the class of 2000.

As you heard earlier, as the Executive Director of the Black Leadership Forum, Inc., informally known as "BLF," I work with and for the twenty-six most prominent African American leaders who are the CEOs of America's best known and most prominent civil rights and service organizations. Many of these leaders are icons, their names emblazoned on the billboards of historic achievements, their contributions to America and to African American progress is unparalleled in our nation's annals. Dr. Joseph E. Lowery; Dr. Dorothy Irene Height; Rev. Jesse L. Jackson; Dr. C. DeLores Tucker; the Honorable Shirley Chisholm; Congressional Black Caucus's James Clyburn and Maxine Waters; former Mayor David Dinkins; and The Joint Center for Political and Economic Studies, Eddie N. Williams, are just a few BLF members and founders. In addition, there are black leaders whom BLF has honored and included into our hall of fame of founders and "lamplighters:" Congressman Charles B. Rangel; Vernon Jordan, Reverend Leon Sullivan; the Honorable Secretary Togo West (your commencement speaker last year), Secretaries Alexis Herman, Hazel O'Leary, Rodney Slater; Philadelphia Bank President Dr. Emma C. Chappell, the late Mrs. Daisy Bates, Judge Constance Baker Motley and Secretary William Coleman. The consolidated list of these Black Leadership Forum leaders is long. Yet, there also are other names which you should recognize but most likely do not: raise your hands if they are familiar to you: Diane Nash; E. D. Nixon; Charles Hamilton Houston; Bob Moses; Fred Shuttlesworth; Septima Clark; Gloria Richardson; and Bill Meek. These leaders, most of whom have at least and, at last, been recognized by the United States Library of Congress, are indeed "profiles in courage from the civil rights movement." Their lives and contributions in large measure explain why Cheney University and most of the other HBCUs remain viable today in spite of adversities in and around the black communities across the country and often within and around the very institutions themselves. So when I spoke with many BLF members, asking them what messages they would have me personally deliver to you today, they, too, were inspired by their own lives and by the lives of many who went before them.

These are their greetings and their lamp posts to light your way as you commence your life's journeys into the twenty-first century:

Dr. Lowery advises you that "love embraces justice." If you cannot love yourself and, through loving yourself, love the least of your brothers, you cannot then demand justice for yourself. Langston Hughes has poignantly reminded us that:

There's a dream abroad in the land with its back against the wall; to save that dream for one, it must be saved for all.

Dr. Lowery says that "love" and "justice" are equal opportunity entitlements.

Dr. Dorothy Irene Height, speaking from the vantage of her eighty-eight years of life and leadership, admonishes you that we each must lift as we climb. That the ladder of achievement will remain steady only so long as there is support from the bottom. This is a practical rule, finding current expression in the class action suits being brought by corporate minorities and women who have alleged that, even as the top ranks of leadership showcased prominent African Americans and women, the ranks at the bottom often have been neglected and ignored by everyone at the top. Black corporate leaders have been hurt by these allegations because if they have not been a part of the solution, they then are seen as having been a part of the problem.

Eddie N. Williams, BLF founding member and president of The Joint Center for Political and Economic Studies, the premier, the first and the only think tank in the country devoted to research for and about the black community, drafted this special message just for you:

> The best advice I can give to any graduating class is to be prepared. Be prepared to meet the many challenges that lie ahead; to seize the opportunities at-hand; to contribute to the success of our people, our communities and our nation. And above all, be prepared for a life time of learning and active participation in the governance of our society.

Mr. Williams's message is a perfect prelude to the continuing theme of Dr. C. DeLores Tucker's life:

You cannot win the prize if you refuse to play the game. Invest in corporations where you wish for your voice to be heard and your values respected. Run for office in communities where your leadership can be better than that currently being provided. Put your money and your abilities where your mouth is, and always vote. Vote early. Vote often. Vote in every single election, no matter how regular or irregular.

Cultures depend upon institutions and traditions for the perpetuation of their values and strengths. If you, many of whom have selected the private sector as the target of your ambitions, do not use your own rich earnings and resources to support institutions which preserve values that inspired this university in 1837, those values will not survive. It is not someone else's responsibility. It is primarily African Americans responsibility for the survival of African American institutions.

From my own vantage, and as a result of my rich daily exposure throughout my life to the lessons of leaders like these and the demands of leadership, I will add to this list of rules to live by: Always look a gift horse in the mouth. When you are told or you read that, as Archie Bunker says "regular Americans" have suddenly become so accepting of blacks that there is a large, new and growing category of mixed race people requiring a separate count by the U.S. Census, raise questions. Be skeptical. Remember that by historical precedent, by virtue of the shameful slavery dynamic and legacy, and therefore, by definition, the label African American, which was preceded by Negro, which was preceded by colored. The label African American means "mixed race." Think about it. Racial mixture pervades the entire history, etiology and fabric of our lives since the census began. It is not new.

Then go and look at research statistics. The numbers are clear. The great rise in interracial marriages is not black with white, or black with any other group. The great increase in interracial marriage numbers and percentages is in the category labeled: "Other interracial married couples, besides blacks and whites, whites with others, and Hispanics and Asians with others." Things are not always as they seem.

Remember also that if you were born and raised here in this county, you are an American. Uniquely American. This is not a gift, it is a reality. Always look a gift horse in the mouth. You do not have any more in common with people on another continent, of another culture, or another language, than you have with people on another continent, of another culture and another language whom you consider to be foreign to yourself. Do not permit anyone, including your own romanticized view of where your "roots" are, to deprive you of your just American inheritance, your entitlement to inclusion, your birthright. You are an American, and that concept may be flawed. But look carefully at the alternative. Always look a gift horse in the mouth.

Live in ways which enrich your soul. Dr. Height says "the BMW in not the goal." The BMW is just the vehicle and the symbol. I add that the soul is the sacred payload. The body is just the delivery vehicle, even when it rides in a BMW or a Lexus.

The soul is patterns of memories, of warm recall and quiet reveries. The soul is the compass which rides above the rapid currents, nudging us always back on course when we take unattractive tributaries and drift off course. The soul is the genesis of warm waves of inspiration and uplifting floods of idealism. The soul is the payload which rests in the watchful penumbra of our life's-odyssey and is called forth by the Classics Poet Dante, who wrote in a verse often recalled by Professor

George A. Johnson, a faculty member here in the late 70s and Professor Ross's grandfather. In *Inferno* Dante wrote:

> In the middle of the journey of our life
> I found myself in a dark wood,
> For I had lost the right path.

But then, Dante implies, the human soul, ever vigilant, arose. And, Dante concludes:

> And so we came forth, and once again beheld the stars.

African American poet, author, iconoclast and feminist scholar, bell hooks, finds soul satisfaction through expression in poetry, as I do. She says, simply, that A poetry sustains life.@ Poetry sustains the soul and often, a useful, purposeful life can be made into poetry. That is your job, as you begin again from a new plateau, remembering that things are not always as they seem.

My closing story is of a gentle black man who drove a large tractor trailer and pulled into a rest stop to eat. He parked and went into the diner, ordering a cheeseburger, a slice of apple pie and a cup of coffee.

Just then, three Hell's Angels, also roared into the rest stop, parked, and went into the restaurant, just as the waitress was bringing the truck driver his order. As she passed them, one biker reached and took the cheeseburger, one reached and took the slice of pie and the third biker took the truck driver's coffee. Then very quietly, the truck driver spoke to the waitress, who was quite distressed, saying: "That's O.K. ma'am, how much was the bill?" He paid the waitress and left the restaurant without another comment.

The bikers laughed raucously, and said to the waitress. "Boy, that guy sure was a wimp. He really wasn't much of a man, was he?"

The waitress shrugged, and said: "Well, I don't know whether he is much of a man or not, but he certainly isn't much of a driver. He ran right over three motor cycles as he pulled out of the rest stop."

Remember that things are not always what they seem.

The Next Millennium: Second Verse of the Dream

"There's a dream out in the land with its back against the wall; to save the dream for one, it must be saved for all…."

—Langston Hughes

It is not personal, this abhorrence which we have for vengeance, vindictiveness and voyeurism. It is enlightened self-interest.

I have been haunted by this verse during the past months, first subliminally, then consciously, and then obsessively. So obsessed have I been with this poem that, for a frightening few moments, I thought that I too had become afflicted with *Capitol Hill Fever*, infected by the same disease which has gripped the House of Representatives' Trial Managers by their senses, stifling rational thought and speech, and fixing their glazed pupils on one hypnotic but illusive goal, the failed removal from office of President William Jefferson Clinton.

For me, also, my goal had been illusive. I have needed to find the part of the verse which was, until this past weekend, lost to my memory. I felt the burn of the verse's first words in my very center: "There is a dream out in the land, with its back against the wall." These words embodied the passion, the urgency, the embattled posture which so many of us have been experiencing in recent years, as once trusted standards of fairness, and accepted strategies to achieve equity and parity, one by one have come under attack, and have often, in fact, been defeated.

But it was not until this past weekend, when a good friend obtained for me the last two lines of the verse, that I realized that these previously lost words: " To save the dream for one, it must be saved for all" were the words which actually have been haunting me. I have been obsessing about the subliminal meaning of the verse <u>in its entirety,</u> even though I could not consciously recall it completely. It had, rather, become embedded over time in my DNA. It represents the essence of my visceral reality and longing, the essence of my subconscious, my subliminal assessment of where we now, in the last year of the twentieth century, find ourselves:

> There is a dream out in the land,
> With its back against the wall;
> To save the dream for one,
> It must be saved for all.

In many respects, this is the answer to the question which many African Americans have been asked repeatedly of late. There is great puzzlement that, given President Clinton's Gethsemane and his crisis of inappropriate behavior, the bulk of the black community has remained steadfastly in opposition to the unfairness and the arbitrariness of the process which led to his impeachment and which, today, occasions his trial by the U.S. Senate. But the answer has been rather direct and transparent for many.

If innocent until proven guilty is the American standard; if the sanctity of grand jury testimony is a democratic guarantee; if the protections of personal privacy are the promise of our Constitution; if hounding and character assassination are not legitimate avenues to fairness, then African Americans—who personally and vicariously live under the daily threat of all of these violations—have no alternative but to stand against these behaviors, no matter where they arise. If we permit them for anyone, these excesses will be applied to everyone. If they are applied to anyone, they most certainly will be applied to African Americans, who are heirs to arbitrariness of the most egregious kinds, whose Constitutional protections are notoriously situational. We know from bitter experience that "to save the dream for one, it must be saved for all."

It is not personal, this abhorrence which we have for vengeance, vindictiveness and voyeurism. It is enlightened self-interest. To protect our dream of fairness for us all, we must protect that dream even for Presidents as well.

Today, in many obvious and discouraging ways, our dream of simple fairness and Constitutional protection is out in the land, with its back against the wall. The three-ringed theater, which has been chronicled ad infinitum and ad nauseam in the media, has inadvertently ungloved the concealed hand of injustice and prejudice and has revealed its face. For African Americans long have known that, as the late Secretary Patricia Roberts Harris used to say, "Just because we're paranoid does not mean that they're not out to get us."

The channeled vision abridgement of rights and protections; the distortion of evidence by a cabal of legal maneuverers; the wanton disregard for facts, and the twisting of these facts to fit obsessive foregone conclusions, are the strategies which our enemies have always used. If these tactics can succeed against the most powerful man in the world, what chances do the less powerful, the disenfranchised, have? An article in yesterday's (2/8/99) *Washington Post* traces a growing dilemma resulting from activist juries who revolt against laws which they see as unjust or unfair. In so doing, they challenge the very basis of American jurisprudence and create a "Recipe for Anarchy." The article asserts:

> The right to a trial by a fair and impartial jury is fundamental in
> America and rests on the belief that a jury may be the only shield

between an individual and an overzealous prosecutor or a biased judge. ... But if the process in breaking down, ...[I]t may suggest that there is something wrong with a central component of American democracy. ...In some cases, ...charges have been brought against jury nullification activists who encourage jurors to "vote your conscience."

This phrase, "vote your own conscience" has become a mantra for the House Trial Managers. They seem to have abandoned all obligations to everyone and everything—including the constitution and the law— just to have the chance to vote their own consciences. Meanwhile, the dream (of fairness) is out in the land with its back against the wall.

Black History Month is Important
This event today marks the Library of Congress' last African American History Month observance for the twentieth century. As most of you know, the observance was first begun by the richly contributing African American scholar, Carter G. Woodson, who also founded the American Association for the Study of Negro Life and History, which continues today as well. He originally promoted a "Negro History Week." Back in the day, as we old civil rights warriors say, we referred to Dr. Woodson as a "Race Man," meaning that the promotion of black race awareness was his priority. Woodson selected a week in February for reflecting on African Americans whose contributions were too little known, because February included the birthdays of both Frederick Douglass and also President Abraham Lincoln.

In 1976, as a natural outgrowth of the emerging political power and influence of the African American community (remember that African Americans were the deciding voters who gave Jimmy Carter the victory as President of the United States that year) the annual celebration of African American history and contributions was extended to a full month, as we continue to do this year.

I always have emphasized that the blood, sweat and tears of our slave ancestors soaked the earth with richness and fertilized the economy to make America the great nation that it is today. But I do not believe that this knowledge of our uncompensated labor and hard-scrabble sacrifices for our country are appreciated widely enough to eliminate the need for Black History Month. My Mother used to remind me, when I lobbied for some Children's Day indulgence—that Children's Day, unlike Mother's Day and Father's Day—was every day! Well, for this Country, Black History Month ought to be every month! But it is not. And so we must continue to invest in February.

When many of you gather here again next year, the new millennium will already have begun. We will carry forward into the next century much of which we can be proud, but also much of which America is as a continuing work-in-progress. We shall, in other words, have an opportunity to begin again, the "second verse of the dream," to try to rescue it from embattlement, to help it achieve its promise. And there are, indeed, elements of the dream which are no longer deferred, which we must transport into the next century with pride.

American Government Has Begun to Look Like America
Today, America's federal government has really begun to look like our communities across the land...to look like America. I have often become impatient when those whom I believe ought to know better, minimize this accomplishment. In my view, the arrival of almost 800 African Americans in significant positions of authority since 1992, is a seismic accomplishment. It is not, as some cynics assert, simply evidence of the opportunities afforded to a selected few who are thus lifted a bit higher into the middle class.

I have concluded that it must be considered "cool" or as my generation used to say, "blasé" to express skepticism about the importance of having minorities particularly African Americans and Latinos in the President's Cabinet and in the very top positions in public and governmental organizations. But, quite to the contrary, the penetration of the top ranks of policymaking has produced a multiplier effect within these organizations, opening heretofore unheard of avenues to valued decisions, resources, and participation in the distribution of access and benefits to those who usually have not been included in these opportunities.

The objective of democracy has always been to activate the promise of equal rights and parity. Civil Rights advocates and other desegregationists have promoted the concept of gaining a place at the table of justice. The commanding image of equity has projected a tableaux in which citizens stand within **all** ranks, at **all** levels of society, participating "from each according to his (or her) own abilities, to each according to his (or her) own needs. (Karl Marx, "Critique of the Gotha Program," 1875.)

Why, then is it not self-evident, that the more people there are who look like all of America, in all of the important places in America, the more of all Americans will be included where once they were not ? It clearly has been established that many positions have opened up to minorities and women when minorities and women finally filled the top decision making positions. Moreover, the values, priorities, cultural contributions and points of view of African Americans, men and women and other minorities have made a significant impact on the institutions in which they have served. We must come to understand that racism, in all of its institutional forms, will yield only to comprehensive initiatives.

Yes, the presence of blacks does matter in the assault on racism. And, yes, the enforcement of laws also matters. And yes, the provision of other remedies matters as well. So, the answer clearly is: All of the above are tremendously important elements of the cure.

The Race Initiative Was A Great Idea

The notion of a President-sponsored Race Initiative was a really great idea. It still is. I regret, however, that the mandate to President Clinton's Advisory Board on Race has expired and that their report is finished. While the Board existed, interested citizens engaged in spirited and revealing debates—both public and private—and established a new high for examination of the thorny, uniquely American dilemma of the color line. Even when transparent motives distracted discussion from the central theme of racial reconciliation and how to achieve it, the compensating sincerity of most ordinary Americans, about eliminating bias and discrimination, was its own reward in this increasingly multi-cultural, multi-colored, multi-racial national hodgepodge.

Unfortunately, now that Dr. John Hope Franklin, Executive Director Judith Winston, Esq. and their Advisory Board colleagues have punctuated their commendable work with a written report, I expect a status quo ante pall to smother efforts to continue a universal dialogue on racism. The report, as richly instructive as it is, will be shelved and the topic will be out-of-sight, out-of-mind. The incentive to examine the contemporary expressions of historic predicates to prejudice, most surely will surrender to shallow rationalizations and indifferent comparisons, mostly between the assimilation rates of later-arriving people of color and the stagnating assimilation of most African American descendants of slaves. Since people usually do not read reports, and the press usually writes in sound bites, I expect that the Advisory Board's conclusions will be largely unfamiliar to Archie Bunker's "regular Americans," who did, in fact, pay some attention to the town meetings and public deliberations of the Advisory Board when it was still alive. The President's Initiative is now a report. It is no longer a process. America is the poorer for that.

Dr. Franklin has characterized the Advisory Board's process as "Talking, not shouting, about race," and the Board tried to set a measured pace. Indeed, the impatience of media critics for a quick fix began when the Board was less than three months into its process. So now reporters will dust off their hands and turn their attention to livelier arts. Yet, ambiguities of unbelievable complexity, still remain largely unexamined, in public discourse as well as in the report, because it takes more than the one year allotted to the Advisory Board to untangle four centuries of racial animus and subjugation.

Take the falsely reassuring matter of "...the increasing amount of interracial marriages," for example. This issue is a ticking stealth bomb waiting to explode the myth of a "beige"—neither black nor white twenty-first century America. Michael Lind writes, in a recent *New York Times* article: "By the end of the next century, experts predict, racial intermarriage will break down the color divide in America. The truth is much darker." The generality of the Advisory Board report's language: "Further complicating the discussions of race is the increasing amount of interracial marriages...." indeed disguises a profound difference in perspective between African Americans and other people of color, as well as tensions within the African American community.

What are the facts in this situation? Reynolds Farley, of the Russell Sage Foundation, has analyzed 1990 Census data for the twenty-five to thirty-four-year-age cohort. He found that 31.6 percent of native-born Hispanic husbands and 31.4 percent of native born Hispanic wives had white spouses. For Asians, the figures are even more dramatic and show that Asian wives are as likely to have white American husbands as they are to have Asian husbands—a 50/50 probability.

And what of the racial conundrum, the one which bridles and harnesses, chokes and inflames efforts to confront racial reality? What about blacks' marriages to everyone else? Michael Lind reports:

> Black-white marriages have risen from a reported 51,000 in 1960 (when they were still illegal in many states) to 311,000 in 1997 (e.g. of 12 Million in the same age cohort or 02.5%). Marriages between white men and black women, although still uncommon, rose from 27,000 in 1980 to 122,000 in 1995. Although black out-marriage rates have risen, they remain much lower than out-marriage rates for Hispanics, Asians and American Indians. For the 25 to 34 age group, only 8 percent of black men marry outside their race. Less than 4 percent of black women do so.

Well, it's all obviously better than it used to be, this process of racial fading-to-beige. But it will be a very long time before the overwhelming number of African Americans will appear to be anything other than African Americans. There is no avoidance in delay. We must get on with the business of racial reconciliation, we must dump the useless concept of colorblindness, and we must value each other for exactly who we are, not who we are fading into.

Maybe, as the U.S. Census data shows, large numbers of Hispanics and Asian Pacific Americans increasingly are "intermarrying" with others— mostly whites—leading to the conclusion that greater tolerance of difference and blurring of ethnicity will result. But African Americans clearly always have been a reflection of blending and mixing. Just look at any two of us. Yet, even the "blended" African American is indiscriminately boxed-in, regardless of the visible degree of blending, by the equal Black-opportunity barriers of the glass ceilings, brick walls, cement floors and steel doors of discrimination. We need more than just one year and a written report to sort out that and other dynamics. I, for one, yearn for and dream of, more openness and fairness in reaching a rapprochement—a reconciliation—about race. I do not really know what being colorblind means, other than the optical pathology which makes some people think that blue is green...or whatever. I do not want to live in a color blind society. There is nothing of greater beauty to me than the tableaux which I see before me today, an array of skin tones, each reinforcing the beauty of the other.

But, even more importantly, I do not want the legacy of my fore parents' contribution to this country to be erased. Slaves were African, at least at the beginning of American slavery. The blood, the sweat and the tears of which I spoke earlier were the ultimate price which we paid for our inalienable rights as fully credentialed Americans. I want our mutual American and African American efforts to comprehend this legacy, to be substantive enough that finally, blacks will no longer need to punish whites for slavery, and whites will no longer continue to punish blacks for slavery. Think about that. There is symmetry there, but the concepts are not an exactly matched pair.

The Devolution of Affirmative Action
Another piece of baggage which will be dragged into the twenty-first century will be a growing schism within the country about the legitimacy and the importance of Affirmative Action. It would help, of course, if we were all at least talking about the same elements and strategies when we use the words Affirmative Action. Instead, the Affirmative Action opponents employ hot-button code words like "preferences" and "quotas" just to enflame the discussion, even though these critics know full well that these are illegal practices and are not Affirmative Action at all.

Other revisionist distort history by claiming that Dr. Martin Luther King, Jr. really did not support Affirmative Action because he was more interested in "the content of our character." (It seems that I always get reminded of this so-called admonition from Dr. King whenever I am in someone's face, demanding my rights.) I wish that I could make every charlatan who uses Dr. King to attack Affirmative Action, learn by heart and recite on demand Dr. King's entire "I Have a Dream" speech. Maybe then they would get it right.

Those who are our guides and gurus in this Affirmative Action battle, especially Renee Redwood of Americans for a Fair Chance, caution us that the field of engagement has changed. We shall no longer be able to delay the enactment of hostile anti-affirmative action congressional legislation by descending upon the House of Representatives and clogging the halls outside of the Judicial Committee's hearing room. And for those who were not there and have heard only propaganda about that encounter, the overwhelming numbers of just barely disciplined activists and leaders succeeded in scaring the daylights out of our cowardly opponents just by our massive presence. The House Committee rapidly tabled the Canady legislation indefinitely. There was no epiphany. There was simply a tactical withdrawal. But we cannot be effective if we continue to challenge threatening legislation at the last minute with too little, too late.

The hired gun and poster boy for the assault on Affirmative Action, Ward Connerly (like a man of color in ethnic camouflage) is the conduit for millions of dollars of funds that are targeted to the state level, not Congress, to turn back the clock on Affirmative Action; this was the designated purse for Proposition 209, the so-called California Civil Rights Initiative. He also fronted the bankroll for Washington State's Initiative 200. He tried to prevail in Houston, but was defeated because the advantage of deceptive language—such as calling the re-enslavement measure a civil rights law was snatched from him by a powerful coalition.

What must be transported into the twenty-first century is the overarching concept that Affirmative Action is not dead. It is alive and well and has been reversed in only two out of three state ballot initiatives. The foes have been capturing the language with the help, sometimes intentional, sometimes inadvertent, of the media. Americans for a Fair Chance believe that a strong message must be developed, recognizing that Affirmative Action is about all Americans, including women as well as minorities. We must bolster Affirmative Action and put a face on it by identifying beneficiaries. We must draft alternative language for ballot initiatives or legislation to clarify that, as most Americans support, Affirmative Action is about opportunity, access, fairness and equity. We must build a war chest of funds which will permit us to communicate all of these things quickly and in a timely fashion. And, most importantly, we must monitor events in California and Washington so that the American people can really see the devastating impact which 209 and 200 are having on diversity in colleges, universities and in the workplace.

The battle fields of our next Affirmative Action encounters which will occur during the next century, will be: Michigan, Colorado, Nebraska, Arizona, New York, North Carolina, New Jersey and Indiana. Other states are reviewing their options.

The Second Verse of the Dream
There is other baggage with valuable contents which we must not leave behind. Voter participation, Census 2000 representation and their corollaries, redistricting, reapportionment and resource distribution are

agenda items of tremendous importance. These issues will make the transition into the twenty-first century turbulent and tense. In some respects, we usher in the new millennium on some of the same notes that accompanied black and white Americans into the twentieth century, when the dream was illusive and ephemeral, seeming, as reconstruction oozed over us, to be quickly receding from grasp. Few in that era gave more careful thought or expressed more insightfully the complexity of our perceptions and dreams of equality than Alain LeRoy Locke, the precocious intellectual and philosopher, who was inspired by his hope for eliminating the "...false conceptions of race (which were)... an obstacle to modern progress and a menace to modern civilization."

Writing just after the turn of the century, in the seminal work *Race Contacts and Interracial Relations*, Professor Locke rejected the idea, as many do today, "that the solution to the racial problem required that we de-emphasize race in modern life and assimilate ethnic groups totally into the dominant American Stock." (And it was a good thing that he did reject it. Clearly, 100 years hence, that still is not about to happen.)

Locke did, however, believe that although race was not necessarily a permanent biological entity (or otherwise totally irrelevant), he wished to retain the concept of race, saying that "people often possessed a race or group sense that contributed to group esteem and power." Here at the end of the century, we have established that to be true, without equivocation. In spite of the deconstructionist assaults by book writers such as Herrnstein and Murray (*The Bell Curve*); D'Souza (*The End of Racism*); Sleeper (*Liberal Racism*); or Stephan and Abigail Thernstrom (*America in Black and White*), some Americans have become adept at weeding out the charlatans, identifying the true believers, and staying on message about the importance of racial honesty.

Just as important, we need to keep the dream of fairness and equity alive. It's out there, embattled but keeping its back against the wall. I believe that there are those of us, "handful that we are," as Langston Hughes lamented, who will dare: To save the dream for one, [So that *we* can] save the dream for all.

"Dream of Freedom"
There is a dream in the land with its back against the wall, by muddled and strange names sometimes the dream is called.

There are those who claim this dream for theirs alone, a sin for which we know they must atone.

Unless shared in common like sunlight and like air the dream will die for lack of substance anywhere.

The dream knows no frontier or tongue, the dream no class or race, the dream cannot be kept secure in any one locked place.

This dream today embattled with its back against the wall; to save the dream for one, it must be saved for ALL—our dream of freedom!
(Langston Hughes, "Dream of Freedom")

A Passion for Progress and Parity

The school, along with just enforcement of the laws, remains the ultimate
equalizer of inequities and the consummate leveler of the playing field.

President Dawson; Dr. and Mrs. President; very Reverend Father
Johnson and very Reverend Dean McKeachie, of my own faith;
Honorable public officials; Distinguished faculty and staff; college
trustees; valued students, and fellow visitors. Good morning.

Thank you, my friend and distinguished President Leonard Dawson,
for your warm and welcome invitation to me to share this, the 101st
Founder's Day Convocation of Voorhees College, with your community.
The gracious hospitality shown me by your charming and gifted wife
and partner Dr. Laura Dawson, and also by you and your colleagues,
has been an oasis of calm and tranquility in the ocean of irrelevant and
obsessive turmoil in which I regularly swim as I work daily in this
nation's capitol, in Washington, D.C. I am grateful for the respite here
in Denmark, South Carolina.

Much of that which we Washingtonians hear in our daily discourse
comes from the halls of the Congress of the United States, where certain
traditions usually do not find comparison in the regular world outside
of Washington. However, there is one tradition with which I began to
associate Voorhees College and the tenure of President Dawson as I
toured this beautiful, expansive and luscious campus last night. That
concept is called "revise and extend." I believe that this concept has
found tangible expression here in Denmark.

As you have been building the superstructure of this impressive
institution upon the firm foundation of its history, you have revised and

extended. As you have added detail and elaborated the design of the physical plant of Voorhees, you have been determined to revise and extend this institution's heritage. As President Dawson and Dr. Laura Dawson have drawn support from those in your near and close communities, Voorhees College has revised and extended its leadership in the world of higher education. You have much of which to be very proud today and I congratulate the Voorhees College family.

This week has been a week of passion for me. This is, of course, Holy Week, and the jubilation of Palm Sunday is unmatched in the liturgy and pomp of the Protestant Episcopal Church, into which I was confirmed many years ago and of which I remain an active member. At my parish in northeast Washington, D.C., at The Church of Our Savior, the smallish congregation permits, indeed encourages personalizing the passion of Holy Week through songs and intercessions, through ritual and symbols, and, more importantly, through living the anticipated pathos of this Maundy Thursday and the certain final suffering on Good Friday.

For Christians, this is the week of crucifixion, redemption and endurance. The stations of the cross, so often traveled by us in our ordinary, daily lives—assume an even more poignant significance when visited along a trail of thorns, sand, vinegar and inevitable death and resurrection, which so characterize the passion of Easter and of Jesus Christ. I have felt, once again, deeply moved by this passion, which in turn has made me more vulnerable to other companion emotions.

We have memorialized, for the thirtieth year, another death whose redemptive quality is much less evident as we survey the progress in some regards and the retrogression in many other regards in the lives of black people in America. Dr. Martin Luther King, Jr., that iconoclastic rebel, that revolutionary of heroic proportions, that model for global revolts against tyranny and oppression wherever they thrive, is becoming more sanitized, daily, by an errant society wishing to justify their destruction of our inheritance from him, and by the continued denial of the debt which is owed to us by an ungrateful country, for 300-plus years of free slave labor.

Dr. King, this disobedient servant of justice; this defiant champion of equality, is being revised. He is quoted more by the reactionary right to justify their transgressions and to rationalize their penury, than he is quoted by the African Americans, young blacks and youths of color whom we all know. We, who jump up into the face of injustice, who stubbornly push our demands for equity, and who defy the claims, made even by some of our own brothers and sisters, that "God is in his heaven and all is right with the world," we are often chastised for being zealots of whom Dr. King would not approve.

And so, passion roiled with fervor in my breast when I was told during a television debate last week—by a forked-tongued appropriator of Dr. King's words, much out of context and with blatant disregard for facts — that my pro-affirmative action and race-conscious views would not be shared by Dr. Martin Luther King, Jr., if he were alive today. In their efforts to dismantle affirmative action by painting it with their cynical brush, we hear from opponents all along the ideological spectrum—from far right to center—that Dr. King believed the we ought not seek judgment upon the color of our skin, but rather, that we ought to be talking about the *"content of our character."* Of course, I respond: "Well, when you promise to do that, then so will I!" Instead, with great sanctimony, these charlatans of deception and distortion intensify their efforts to eliminate race entirely from any positive consideration for anything, even though we know that most of the time, race is the negative measure of black folks for everything: jobs, housing, promotions, training, school admissions, bussing, contracts for public work. In every arena, in fact, where we have, in the recent past, finally begun to overcome barriers and make advances. Well, with passion today, I remind us all that what Dr. King really said was:

> I have a dream that my four children will one day live in a
> nation where they will not be judged by the color of their skin,
> but by content of their character. I have a dream today.

Today, thirty-five years later, that "dream" of Dr. King's still is a dream, not reality. We have only to study the portrayal of African Americans in the daily press in most towns, to validate this claim. But we will revisit this reality later.

My passion has been activated also during this past week, by a young woman with whom you are familiar, about whom I have learned much lately, and for whom, although she no longer lives, I was greatly and passionately pained. Elizabeth Evelyn Wright, the founder of Voorhees College, then Voorhees Normal and Industrial School, was a woman of deeply held commitments, and of passionate determination to serve young black men and women. I cannot adequately relate to you how distressed I have felt, and how angry I have become, as I have read of Ms. Wright's efforts—thwarted year after year, in town after South Carolina town—to establish the school which flourishes, finally today, as Voorhees college.

The turbulence which her journey stirred within me could hardly be contained. There was much racism, much sexism, much condescension by which she was confronted. But, finally, after four hard years, there was enough caring, loyalty, and genuine commitment from others, black and white, to give realization to Ms. Wright's dream and to create your community as it is today.

Yet, make no mistake about it: there are parallels between the obstacles which she overcame then, and the obstacles which the African American community faces today, as we try to improve public education, to make world-class quality education accessible even to the poorest child in the darkest ghetto, and to make black folks relevant in a still-evolving global world of work.

There is synergy between other experiences of Ms. Wright's, and the experiences which we witness today. For example, the number of school buildings and would-be school buildings which mysteriously went up in flames in the middle of the night, (or maybe it was by spontaneous combustion, do you think? maybe from an overly hot moon?). These so-called "natural disasters" succeeded in delaying education—and maybe even depriving of education, for countless black boys and girls. There were, in 1891, 116,535 African Americans enrolled in South Carolina's public schools (or common schools as they were then called), with a total teaching population of 1,622 working in these common schools in 1891. The student-teacher ratio was 72:1 when Ms. Wright begged pennies, often in vain, from 1893 until 1897 to create this school. Sounds almost like today's urban classrooms, doesn't it?

Similarly, in our times today, the massive infusion of $2 million dollars from reactionary and rightwing conservative opponents to incinerate and destroy Affirmative Action by passing Proposition 209 in California is having a parallel consequence of denying access to public education to African American and Hispanic students. Proposition 209's supporters poured millions of dollars into that referendum, assuring its victory, including the reported $2 million from tabloid newspaper baron and T.V. (FOX) magnet Rupert Murdoch. Especially since donated dollars to defeat Proposition 209 did not even begin to compare with this. Money really not only talked—it screamed.

The results of 209 have been more draconian than even its ardent supporters anticipated. Listen to Korean-born lawyer John Yoo, life-long opponent of affirmative action, former law clerk to Supreme Court Justice Clarence Thomas and Senator Orrin Hatch's general counsel on the senate judiciary committee: "I had no idea what would happen. The numbers had always been available, but I never looked to see what the effect of 209 would be on admissions. I didn't realize the score gaps were so huge."

The results, in fact, have been ominous—for the state of California, for blacks and Hispanics, especially regarding law schools, where statistics are more specific by race than by gender. At Berkeley Law's Boalt Hall, black admissions dropped from seventy-four to fifteen, with only one black student choosing to enroll in 1997. At U.C.L.A. Law, admissions fell from 104 in 1996, to twenty-one in 1997. Only eight students chose to enroll. Lawyer Yoo states further:

> I didn't realize until Proposition 209 went into effect that Affirmative Action, as it was applied by the schools, allowed you to have some racial (and gender) diversity and at the same time to maintain intellectual standards for the majority of your institutions. It was a form of limiting the damage. Now that you have race (and gender) neutral methods, if you still want to get African Americans and Hispanics in, you have to redefine the central mission of the research university in a way that lowers standards for everybody. That's an unintended consequence of 209 and it's unfortunate.

He didn't realize? Unintended? Unfortunate? Excuse me?
The following is from Jeffery Rosen's February 23, 1998, *New Yorker* article:

> Proposition 209, in short, has brought into focus the following question: Is it academically or politically acceptable to define merit in a way that excludes African Americans, (Hispanics and many women) from the most selective public institutions? Lani Guinier, among others, argues that standardized tests, such as the S.A.T. and L.S.A.T., reward speed and strategic guessing over skills that are purportedly more often found in women and minorities, such as story telling and negotiation.

The nationally respected Joint Center for Political and Economic Studies reports, in its December 1997 *Focus Magazine*, in the "Trendsetter" section, that minorities are increasingly discouraged from applying to medical school:

> [T]he number of underrepresented minorities accepted to medical schools across the country this year declined by an alarming 6.8 percent. The (Association of American Medical Colleges) has identified the assault on affirmative action in higher education as the primary reason for the decline and concluded that it is discouraging minorities from pursuing careers in medicine.

This is from *Focus* magazine's, "Trendsetter" November 1996: "According to the Joint Center, AAMC found that in California, Texas, Louisiana and Mississippi, the number of African Americans, Mexican Americans, Puerto Ricans and Native Americans who applied to in-state medical schools was 17 percent lower in 1997 than in 1996. Many interpret these statistics to mean that many minority students just have given up on climbing over these barriers."

But, as Houston wins and Washington (state) gambles not to lose, there is still hope. Forewarned is fore-armed. In Houston, Texas, in November 1997, blacks and Hispanics turned out in large numbers to confirm their support for the city's Affirmative Action Programs in hiring and contracting. But even with strong and active support for newly elected black, Mayor Lee Brown, as well as excellent support from out-going Mayor Bob Lanier and former Mayor Kathy Whitmire (both white,) still, divisions remained in the voting patterns. Most whites voted against Affirmative Action, while most minorities voted for it.

Yet, a strong strategy, building on lessons learned in California on Proposition 209, helped that victory. This accumulating knowledge, in conjunction with the very expensive experience of last minute maneuvering to avoid disaster, which the Piscataway, New Jersey case has provided, will be sorely needed to confront the challenge now being posed by the state of Washington's Initiative 200 (I–200).

Washington State's Initiative 200 Provides: "The state shall not discriminate against, or grant preferential treatment to, any individual of a group on the basis of race, sex, color, ethnicity, or national origin in the operation of public employment, public education or public contracting."

Much of the delicacy—and devil—of I–200 is, of course, in the detail, and in the intent. Like its California inspiration, definitions have been co-opted and appropriated to suit the objectives of its supporters. For example, California's proposition was actually named a "civil rights" law. In the case of Washington's initiative, "preferential treatment" is the "hot button" term.

It is vicious and hypocritical. In a poll conducted by Lou Harris for The Fund for a Feminist Majority in late 1996, it was clearly established by a significant majority of the respondents that Americans are very supportive of "opportunity, access, equity and fairness," which actually characterize Affirmative Action. And, they are just as strongly opposed to "preferences and quota's," both of which are illegal and do not characterize Affirmative Action.

So guess why the term "preferences" was chosen and is being emphasized by the supporters of Proposition 209 and Initiative 200? As I have appeared publicly, I have charged the opponents, mostly white males, with being enamored with the word "preferences" because they, themselves, have enjoyed white male preferences for 300 years. Similarly, I have stated that the obsession with "quotas" derives directly from there having been "quotas" restricting blacks and women since reconstruction.

Dr. Dorothy Height, president emerita of the National Council of Negro Women, tells of her acceptance at Barnard College only to be denied enrollment because "We already have our one colored student for this class."

But members of the pro-affirmative action coalition, led by Ms. Renee Redwood, of Americans for a Fair Chance, offer the following, unpublished summary analysis:

> Although it is difficult to predict with exact certainty the full impact that Initiative 200 would have on Washington law given its vague and ambiguous language, the plain meaning of the term preference would appear to prohibit nearly all state and local programs aimed at increasing opportunities for women and minorities, including

recruitment, training and outreach programs in public education, employment and contracting. Particularly given the list of programs that Governor Wilson considers to be eliminated by Proposition 209, it would appear that even attempts to increase the number of minority applicants in public universities and to encourage women and minorities into careers in which they are under-represented would be prohibited by initiative 200.

In many respects, the courageous founder of Voorhees College, whose seminal legacy you celebrate today, was a race and gender pioneer. In fact, it is interesting to note, in reading Elizabeth Evelyn Wright's biography and the history of Voorhees, that her place as a role model was not fully appreciated during her lifetime. It is reported that following her untimely death, Voorhees experienced a most distressing period of transition, particularly with regard to hiring a suitable director for the school because, and I quote: "[T]he most difficult task [was] in getting a man to fill [the job] satisfactorily." Perhaps Ms. Wright should have left a note for the search committee: If *your* gender doesn't work, try *mine*.

Clearly, her role in advancing worthy educational goals for African Americans was historic. If in no other way, this institution stands, over 100 years later, as testimony to that contribution. But there are indeed, other indications of the merit of Ms. Elizabeth Evelyn Wright's educational philosophy, and of the vision which she and Dr. Booker T. Washington defended, even as this vision was trampled in the bloody battle of industrial versus liberal arts education. It is said that "truth stamped to earth will rise again."

Today, in international research and collaborations to solve the vexing problem of un-employment and under-employment, a reincarnation of the century-old concept of vocational education finds currency under the new names, "apprenticeship programs" and "school-to-work initiatives." Booker T. Washington's original model, which found exact replication here at Voorhees through founder Wright, was the keystone to vocational education. Its history in the United States, however, was not universally respected. As a result, refinement and revision into an effective contemporary model has been constrained, thus seriously impeding any real adaptation of youth training programs that are succeeding in foreign countries.

A few years ago, a study by the Joint Center for Political and Economic Studies included an assessment of selected apprenticeship programs in Germany, Denmark and Sweden.

The indications are reported as follows: (this appeared in *Focus Magazine*: April 1993 on page five:)

> [T]he reason two-thirds of German youth enter apprenticeship programs is two-fold: The programs are viewed positively by society and young apprentices. [And the young] are rewarded for their efforts by the marketplace.

> In the United States, by contrast, vocational education programs are viewed as dumping grounds for students who are not considered "college material." Wide spread acceptance here of vocational training as a valued option, [therefore] will depend on whether this society can broaden its view of this form of education and see it as having equal value with a college preparatory curriculum.

I can imagine that Voorhees will explore the option of tapping into the recent $45 million dollar three-year gift to the United Negro College Fund, to transfer some of this institution's rich knowledge of work-based education to public school districts which are seeking solutions to, and models for, reinventing their educational programs. As historically black and other more vulnerable two and four-year academic institutions are challenged to reach beyond their physical boundaries and into their surrounding communities for mutual benefit, it is inevitable that joint ventures with new charter schools and other pragmatic feeder-school models will be appealing to both town and gown.

Voorhees's "smarts" is an excellent example of a model for effective and successful welfare reform. Another model currently enjoying great success is the Samuel Dewitt Proctor Academy Charter School in West Trenton, New Jersey. In collaboration with my alma mater the University of Pennsylvania, with Yale University, and the College of New Jersey, and supported by city, state, public, business, foundation and other private funds, this residential year-round, full-day academy portends a cutting edge future for public secondary and post-secondary education. It sounds to me a lot like Ms. Wright's dream. Clearly she was onto something much ahead of her time. Thus, when cavalier conservatives—touting the marvelous gifts of "educational choice" and of an educational voucher-happy black community, I recall with appropriate passion, the hard work, dedication, daunting miles to be hiked, and investments needed to achieve this nirvana. The life experiences of Elizabeth Evelyn Wright are relived many times over as budget cuts and other distracting tactics try to push quality, accessible and affordable education once again "out of the reach of the masses," as Ms. Wright often lamented.

A $17,000.00 per pupil annual cost for a charter school, like New Jersey's academy, sounds astronomical until we remember that it costs over $30,000.00 per year to house a single juvenile in prison. On many levels, the obvious choice should be a no-brainer.

In 1893, the year before Ms. Wright embarked upon her pursuit of her dream to build this institution, my paternal grandfather, Dr. Lawson Andrew Scruggs, wrote and published a book. *Women of Distinction: Remarkable in Works and Invincible in Character,* was its name. It is probably in your library here, as it is in the Library of Congress and the libraries of most H.B.C.Us. This book was inspired by women just like Ms. Wright.

Born into slavery in 1857, Grandfather Scruggs also traveled a road of hardship and denigration in pursuit of his dream of helping his people through the practice of medicine. Yet, in his prime, and even as he tried to establish his specialty in respiratory illnesses, his passion for truth drove him to conduct an empirical study of the achievements of 100 African American women. He wrote in his preface to *Women of Distinction*:

> [I]t is quite evident that the world has not as yet learned to fully appreciate the extent to which mind and character have been and can be developed in the women of this race. ...[T]hese glorious days that we now enjoy are made more sacred when we remember the sacrifices, the tears, the labors, the prayers and the blood of thousands of our mothers and sisters, most of whom have gone into another world, but some of whose triumphs are herein mentioned.

I suspect that were Grandfather alive today, he might, in retrospect, modify that claim of "glorious days." Nonetheless, in addition to profiling ninety-one African American women in his 382–page book, more than half of them educators and school builders, my grandfather founded the first (so far as we know) tuberculosis sanitarium for African Americans at Southern Pines, North Carolina. In his book, he included a familiar and famous verse, which I shall paraphrase and with which

I shall close, reminding us all that the school, along with just enforcement of the laws, remains the ultimate equalizer of inequities, and the consummate leveler of the playing field. Ms. Elizabeth Evelyn Wright certainly knew that instinctively, and would agree with the adjustments which I have made in this verse, I am sure: "Great statesmen govern nations, Kings mould a people's fate; but the thirst for truth and wisdom these giants regulate. The ponderous wheel of fortune in colleges is pearled; for the 'she' possessing knowledge, is the 'she' that rules the world."

May God bless us all in the challenges that lie ahead.

Racism and Racial Inequality

Racism has endured because the American resolve has been lacking.

There is a single major threat to the internal sanity, the emotional strength and the moral endurance of the American republic as we approach a new century. That threat is racism and the racial inequality it produces as it continues to persecute American blacks as its primary target and, as though through reflected hostility, to undermine the status of other peoples of color in America. Racism and racial inequality are the contaminating legacy of a uniquely American version of the ancient, barbaric institution of slavery.

Slavery, although officially discontinued well over a century ago, is the defining historic antecedent to the still persisting subjugated status of American blacks as this century ends. To deny this baseline reality of the black-white experience, as too many Americans defensively persist, is to condemn American racial reconciliation to abject failure. To insist that the condition of slavery was "then" and that its harness does not reach into "now" to yoke both white and black to a superior-inferior hierarchy of assumed race-worth and race-worthlessness, is to deny the reality of cultural transmission. To dismiss as contrived—or worse, irrelevant—this yet—unameliorated dimension of the tense black-white dichotomy in America, is to invest heavily in the perpetuation of racism and racial inequality. It is this vicious circle of denial which must now be broken if our republic is to avoid failure.

Racism and racial inequality have endured beyond the shift in the American economy from agricultural, to an industrial one no longer dependent upon slavery for its advancement; beyond two World Wars, each vividly demonstrating this nation's dependence upon all of its

116

diverse human resources in order to prevail. Beyond the Korean Conflict and the later Vietnam War; beyond decades of immigration of those whose rightful transportation, from newcomers into the mainstream, has been enthusiastically expedited, in contrast with that of blacks and other minorities of color. Beyond all of these defining moments, racism and racial inequality have endured. Beyond even the cleansing Civil Rights and Voting Rights Laws, the non-violent social action which went before, and the provoked sporadic urban riots of the decades which followed, racial inequality remains America's lingering social and moral deficit.

The French social commentator, Alexis D'Toqueville, predicted the insidious American dilemma of racism before this century began. The African American public intellectual and international scholar W.E.B. Du Bois, warned of this social deficit at the beginning of this century in 1903, when he wrote of America's unresolved "problem of the color line." In subsequent discourse, historian-scholar John Hope Franklin, who became in 1997 the Chair of President Clinton's Race Initiative's Advisory Commission, wrote in his 1976 book, *Racial Equality in America*:

> Equality, as used here, is not only an ancient concept whose roots go back to the Greek republics. It is also a concept deeply embedded in American constitutional law. One either has it or does not have it. Thus, it is scarcely germane to the central point to observe that blacks are better off now than they were a half-century ago or that they are better off here than they are in Zambia or Mauretania. The criterion to measure the status of their equality is...set forth in the Constitution under which they live and the equality enjoyed by others who live under that same Constitution.

Now, at the end of the twentieth century, as racial diversity, racial identity, racial justice and racial self-determination literally and figuratively color major national policy debates and challenge the authenticity of public procedures, the consideration of racism and racial equality is fragmented and diffused. According to Harvard University scholar Henry Louis Gates, Jr., most discussion consists largely of "...a binary discourse of accusation and counter-accusation, of grievance and counter-grievance, of victims and victimizers." In short, although sincere national leadership is emerging, the problem of racism lacks public focus, public commitment and the participation of enough public voices who know what they are talking about.

Too many people "don't get it." The writer, bell hooks, another powerful intellect who long has examined racism through the duo-dimensional prism of black womanhood, has commented in her recent book, *Killing Rage Ending Racism*:

> For some of us talking race means moving past the pain to speak, not getting caught, trapped, silenced by the sadness and sorrow. I find myself reluctant to talk race because it hurts. It is painful to think long and hard about race and racism in the United States. Confronting the great resurgence of white supremacist organizations and seeing the rhetoric and beliefs of these groups surface as part of accepted discourse in every aspect of daily life in the United States startles, frightens, and is enough to throw one back into silence. No one in the dominant culture seems to consider the impact it has on African Americans and people of color in general to turn on radios and televisions, look at magazines and books which tell us information like that reported ...by Andrew Hacker in *Two Nations: Black And White, Separate, Hostile, Unequal*.

There certainly is ample evidence of a turbulent need for structured discourse on racism and racial inequality which, if not self-apologizing or superficial, could lead to intentional and sustained racial reconciliation. President Clinton has galvanized this urgency into a national initiative, inviting every single American to participate. He is to be commended for his leadership and for the quality of those whom he has appointed to serve for one year on his Advisory Commission on Race.

Thinkers from both ends of the ideological spectrum, however, as well as from perspectives well outside both the Left and the Right, have written recent conflicting ideas about racism. *Race Matters* is Cornel West's response to William Julius Wilson's wishful thinking about *The Declining Significance of Race*. Dinesh D'Souza's assertions of blacks feigned victimhood in his book, *The End of Racism*, are challenged by Jewelle Taylor Gibbs's powerful psychoanalysis of California's cognitive dissonance about racism in her book, *Race and Justice*. And legal activist-scholar Derrick Bell inveighs against "...the permanence of racism" reflected in the *Faces at the Bottom of the Well*," the title itself an imagery devastating in its diabolic double-entendre.

Many independent and unilateral efforts also attempt to open the discourse while closing America's growing racial fissure. New Jersey's former U.S. Senator Bill Bradley continues, now privately as he did publicly and officially in the Senate, to alert the country to the threat of unresolved racism.

The Race Relations Institute (RRI) of historically black Fisk University, has seized the initiative, inviting national experts and international advocates against racism to a "New National Dialogue on Race." No doubt the Institute's intense deliberations will be anxiously awaited— even by a press which, more often than not, will extract the most simplistic soundbyte, at the expense of the substantive statement of principle. Thus, once again—as the Kerner Commission observed thirty years ago—the nation will be misled by a media seemingly unable to represent accurately the sum and substance of "truth" for people of color.

The national polls tell a sad story. The Joint Center for Political and Economic Studies has reported recently, based on its biennial national poll in 1997, on opinions and attitudes of 850 black Americans and 850 other Americans—blacks, whites, Hispanics/Latinos and Asians—with a 100 respondent over-sample of Hispanics in recognition of their rapid growth. David Bositis, principal author of the Joint Center's findings, observes that from the perspective of public opinion, the state of race relations in the United States remains troubled. "Black and white perceptions of racial reality, while occasionally convergent, for the most part are quite different. In fact, blacks believe that, in the main, there is "a lot of discrimination against black Americans," and that the perpetrators include the police. Of great importance is the view of both blacks and Hispanics that "not enough attention is paid to discrimination against Hispanics."

The Gallop Organization also conducted a poll which—although methodologically flawed in my opinion, because black interviewers (rather than less threatening whites) asked white respondents sensitive questions about their feelings toward blacks—has nonetheless presented some interesting data on racism. The future prospects for black acceptance by whites in the work place, in their neighborhoods, in their children's schools and into their families through intermarriage—is optimistic and positive, according to the Gallop findings. Some skepticism attends these outcomes, however, given the responses in yet another survey, "Taking America's Pulse" conducted by the National Council (formerly, "...Of Christians and Jews.") Their data shows that African Americans are ranked lowest of all designated races—Protestant whites, other whites, Koreans, Hispanics / Latinos and blacks—in all offered hierarchies of positive perceptions, in the opinions of all designated races surveyed. In other words, according to this poll, blacks are seen as contributing least to American society; being the least devout; and being the least desirable to be hired and given comparability in credentials. Unfortunately, surveyed Blacks themselves also reported that they usually expect to be held in such low regard by the other racial and ethnic groups.

The Fund for a Feminist Majority collaborated with Lou Harris in 1996 to conduct a poll. They found that the negative perception of Affirmative Action by most people is largely a function of such code words as "preferences" and "quotas" used by the surveyors. This does not come as a surprise to those who feel that opposition to Affirmative Action is a thinly veiled longing for the return to centuries-old white male only preferences.

Other polls have also informed our understanding of the racial divide. In the recent past, a *New York Times* poll reaffirmed that, in spite of statistical dispersion of people of color out of the urban core and into suburban and rural America, more groups live separated from each other than ever before. There are balkanized communities where whites never see or have a substantive interaction with blacks from one week to the next, and vice versa. Moreover, their primary source of information about blacks, and most others of color, is from ...guess where ...television! This means the mostly sensational six o' clock news—where failure rather than success reigns. Alternatively, they see one of the several ebonically challenged sitcoms, especially since Bill Cosby's and James Earl Jones's weekly programs depicting successful mainstream blacks are the rare exceptions to current primetime fare.

Native American's have long since been defined in mainstream American's minds by Roy Rogers and Trigger, the Lone Ranger and Tonto, John Wayne, and 100 years of American westerns. Hispanics and Asians have been defined, to everyone's detriment, by the 1990s versions of "West Side Story" and "The World of Suzie Wong."

In other words, most Americans have no reliable, accurate empirical experiences on which to base their conclusions about each other. Thus, both the Gallup Poll and the Joint Center's poll have shown that everybody—blacks, whites, Hispanics and Asians— thinks that there are twice as many blacks as there actually are, half as many whites as there actually are, and more Hispanics and Asians than there actually are. A familiar "conventional wisdom" is apparent: Michael Jordan and other African American athletes dominate basketball and football. Ergo, blacks must be everywhere. And Hispanics are portrayed as such an illegal immigration problem that they must be flying over the transoms and storming the borders by the thousands…as so many, many people believe apparently.

Even still, our dysfunctional national denial of racial inequality also denies a problem-solver like former Justice Department nominee Lani Guinier the opportunity to publicly defend her proposals for diminishing racism through the electoral process. We had better get, and actively use, better information than we seem to have today.

The coloring of America; racial demographics are changing dramatically, by 2050, as the first half of the twenty-first century is over, white Americans will no longer be the traditional, clear majority, and will account for barely 50 percent of the population, not 78 percent as is the case in 1998. African Americans will no longer be the largest minority group, with their numbers rising slightly to barely top 15 percent in 2050. Hispanic/Latinos will constitute one-quarter of all Americans, up considerably from today's 10 percent, and Asian Americans will be as numerous as blacks are today (12 percent). Projections concerning Native Americans are not currently available, but we know that the divide and conquer strategy of white America's westward migration drastically altered the size and shape of Indian communities from "sea to shining sea."

Certainly, based upon the current U.S. Census Bureau's debates about "multi-racial" categories, and the growing non-doctrinaire cross-racial sentiments among younger minorities who probably will be the leaders of 2050, we may well face profound redefinitions of who we all are anyway. That will not, however, relieve the problem of racism for everyone. Instead, unless we begin to celebrate, not dilute, our differences, racism will turn inward, eroding the Nation's center. President Clinton has said that he wants "...to lead the country in a great and unprecedented conversation about race..." He admits that "...honest dialogue may not be easy at first." But he hopes "...that honest dialogue and concerted action will help to lift the heavy burden of race from our children's future."

We need to talk. But racial reconciliation will require more than just talk. Conversations, of course, are important. They humanize the perceptions of race differences, and help to overcome the burden of history. There are those who have felt that the effort should begin with an apology. Canada demonstrated in 1997 when the government issued an apology to the Indians who were displaced, that it does enlarge rather than diminish a nation to say: "We're sorry."

Contrary to the views of opponents of an apology, the Civil War was not an apology to African Americans for slavery. The Civil War was an economic and political conflict, undertaken by white men to determine who among themselves would have hegemony over the government—and how the economic and political vehicle of slavery would control geography. The outcome of the Civil War was an expression of who was stronger, not who was morally repentant to Africans brought to these shores for economic gains.

The Thirteenth, Fourteenth and Fifteenth Amendments, the Civil Rights act of 1964, the Voting Rights Act of 1965, the Great Society's Programs and other well intentioned efforts to address the results of slavery, were not apologies from the American government for slavery. It is true that an apology would be symbolic. But the American flag is symbolic. The National Anthem is symbolic. The Constitution and the Bill of Rights are symbolic. All of these symbols require supporting action to give substantive expression to their intent.

A second reconciliation requirement is the communication of model remedies and examples of successful local initiatives, through a multi-dimensional clearinghouse: verbal, electronic, visual, and experiential. As Dr. Henry Ponder, former President of Fisk University has suggested: "Into the villages, hamlets, towns, countryside and cities, we ought to beam a simultaneous opportunity for every American to become enrolled and invested in this serious dialogue on race." They should be encouraged also to tell their success stories over all of these wavelengths.

A respectful enforcement of existing laws and policies, and maintenance of protections which correct injustices and assure equity both from citizens and law enforcers as well, is a third requirement of racial reconciliation. blacks and Hispanics see daily examples of manipulation of laws which reinforce racial inequality: efforts to eliminate Affirmative Action; the political redistricting to eliminate gains realized by majority-minority districts; and mandatory sentencing for crack possession but not for cocaine distribution, to name a few.

A fourth indispensable dimension to a successful national racial reconciliation initiative is universal access to reliable and relevant facts, information and data. Such information broadly circulated as a high priority, just like the Internal Revenue Service's annual 1040 forms and instruction manual, would keep the dialogue honest, make the conversations realistic, and have everyone reading from the same page in the hymnal—so to speak. A lot of racism is just plain, willful ignorance.

As a national priority, America needs to begin proposing public strategies for harnessing the energy of our diversity and blending it into a force which unifies rather than rends the fabric of our society. Forging a formal national assault on racism seems to me to be just as important as building a national network of twenty-first century volunteers, the subject of the most recent national summit, which the President hosted in 1997.

Still, the President's Initiative on Race has great promise. Contrary to conventional wisdom, the Board is not supposed to be a forum for exposing all of the various divergent views of sundry Americans. Rather, according to Advisory Commission Chair, Dr. Franklin:

> We are trying to tell the President some things we think he can do to improve the conditions of people in this country as they have relations with one another. How much discrimination is there in colleges? How much discrimination is there in the work place? What is the relationship between hate crimes and racial problems? ... We're trying to get people to talk about race. It's a real challenge. People don't want to talk about it because they have never had to.

Black folks inspire a new "cottage industry?" Nonetheless, the main 1998 agenda for civil rights—opportunity, access, fairness and equity—is facing frustrating challenges from right wing reactionaries and determined opponents who are otherwise quite detached from the actual practice of civil rights. Through the obsessive and often misguided scrutiny of African American life and circumstance and with the support of a cynically inspired national publishing network and the media, these opportunists have created a very visible and profitable cottage industry through the study of black folks.

It is reasonable for scholars of any hue or ideology to investigate vexing social, economic and political conditions. But when obscure academics and self-serving opinionators devote inordinate time, resources and attention to "explaining" and "re-defining" black folks and other people of color—in order to demonstrate how little we understand our own condition and how unappreciative we are of the gains which larger society has permitted us—there is ample reason for suspicion. I, for one, am very suspicious about this growing Cottage Industry. It is unlikely that they are inspired by the prospect of a Nobel Prize.

A legitimate question, then, is: Even if their findings were correct, what is the prize which they hope to win? The answer is obvious. The prize will be a return to white male preferences, white male quotas, and a most-favored position for white males which, for over two hundred years in our past, characterized America's social and domestic balance of power.

In fact, these recent revisionist definitions of black reality, passing as research and scholarly study, successfully reinforce arguments against black demands for opportunity, access, equity and justice. The revisionist strategy seeks to deny any further black advancement and if possible, to reverse and systematically eliminate the economic and political gains which African Americans have earned in the last thirty years, often because of support from laws, public policies and court decisions. The books and articles which are the vehicles for the new Cottage Industry are prominently reviewed and aggressively promoted by both mainstream publishers and the mainstream press.

Take, for example, Stephan and Abigail Thernstrom, two such Cottage Industry entrepreneurs. Together they have written a 671–page long and tedious tome, *America in Black and White: One Nation, Indivisible*, based upon their collection and analysis of data in ways which cynically prove exactly what the data has been selected to prove: that African Americans are deceiving everyone by denying that we are "almost" as well off as whites. The Thernstroms further assert that the Civil Rights Act of 1964, the Voting Rights Act of 1965 and Affirmative Action practices of the last thirty years have had little or nothing to do with our progress. It was inevitable, said the Thernstroms, that black conditions would improve—without help from activists, laws or advocates.

Their book is an example of the parasitic quality of the Black Folk Cottage Industry. Two largely unknown, white college teachers, through the manipulation of information, collaboration with a national publishing house (Simon and Schuster) and mainstream media (*The New York Times* and *The Washington Post* among others) have begun to showcase their opinions in primetime and on the front pages of the daily press...above the fold. On invitation from the White House (to Dr. Franklin's chagrin, I am told), they were special guests at the Akron, Ohio Town Meeting of the President's Racism Advisory Commission. The White House released excerpts of their comments during their private discussion with the President. These excerpts accompanied the front page photo opportunities arranged for the White House Press Corps.

Curiously, none of these same attentions accompanied the two-hour long, August 5, 1997, Cabinet Room meeting between the President, the Vice-President, several Cabinet members and fifteen leaders of the Black Leadership Forum. At that meeting, BLF presented the President with eleven specific, written recommendations for helping his Race Commission become substantive. BLF held a press conference (fairly well attended) on the White House lawn afterward, and then sent out news releases over the wire service, specifying the recommendations. In this case, the White House did not issue transcripts on the meeting, and there was no national media coverage at all, not to mention front page photos. There is, indeed, a message here.

Dinesh D'Souza, although himself arguably non-white, joins the Black Folk Cottage Industry through his oft-referenced book, *The End of Racism*. *The Bell Curve* also exhausted much ink, and 663 pages, as authors Herrstein and Murray strove to prove that blacks are genetically inferior. They used test scores to support their assessment, biasing the outcomes of their effort by the analytic tools which they chose.

Unfortunately, I could go on. There are many others whose notions would be gathering appropriate dust on remote university and research offices' shelves were it not for a rich and rewarding Black Folks Cottage Industry. The point is not that many of these authors study and write about people of color, but rather, that what they write is designed to prove—mostly to themselves, I believe—that they have discovered that blacks and others who demand equality and justice, really do not deserve it after all. This sensationalism—like tabloid journalism—guarantees prominence to mediocre intellects, who otherwise would languish in well deserved obscurity.

A twenty-first century Civil Rights strategy—what should be done? An appropriate resolution for the new century by the civil rights community is that the forces for equity and justice, against racism and racial inequality, will once again become the official definer of these terms, since they are most directly and dramatically affected by them. The civil rights community must become very emphatic in defining the policies which effectively offer opportunity, access, fairness and equity. The years since the Laws of 1964 and 1965, and the issuance of the Kerner Commission Report, have verified that the prophet Amos and Dr. Martin Luther King's united entreaty to "Let justice run down like waters and righteousness like a mighty stream," still needs a lot of mortal vigilance.

America can no longer permit Affirmative Action to be a dirty word, to be reinterpreted as the pejorative and diminished concept, as is happening with the term "liberal." These concepts are not passé. Affirmative action is a good thing. It has helped many minorities and women to gain access where denied; to excel where opportunities formerly did not exist; to demand fairness in assessment of their qualifications; and to enjoy equity where white male preference once prevailed. We must claim it and celebrate these values. The accountability of the mainstream press was carefully scrutinized in the original Kerner Commission Report. While press analysis and balanced coverage have continued to improve during the ensuing thirty years, more responsibility must be assigned to the media for racial imaging and accurate portrayal.

Moreover, the local weekly and black press must be given—and must agree to accept—a larger role in communicating constructive and useful information about the strengths and achievements of the African American community, as well as in other communities of color. Perception is reality—for everyone, but especially for children and youth of color. If the only images advanced are negative and uncomplimentary, and these are not balanced and countered with positive, encouraging reports, both people of color and those who do not know better, will accept these images as gospel truth. Therefore, all those who oppose racism—whether white, black or people of color—must insist upon and foster positive images and portrayals.

Capital formation has the single greatest potential for continued progress for most African Americans and people of color. Thus, the black and minority entrepreneurial class must expand. Through this expansion, increased support for mediating institutions can be provided. Mediating institutions include educational institutions, community centers, religious organizations, private and community social service providers, and other helping, training and advocating organizations, which traditionally have provided transport up the social and economic ladder into mainstream America. Unless financial support for these institutions increases, their survival is in jeopardy.

Dr. James Comer, Yale University professor and author of the recent challenge, *Waiting for a Miracle: Why Schools Can't Solve Our Problems and How We Can*, comments:

> There is the question of what kind of country do we want. We are well on our way to being a country of a few privileged and large numbers of people who are locked out of the system. Our posture needs to be turned around so that we systematically...focus on the things what will make it possible for our kids to make it into the mainstream of society. And we can make that case and make it to poor whites as well, if we united around our kids and raise those issues.

Finally, those who value true democracy, civil rights and justice, must take on the "war room" mentality. Let no lie go unchallenged. Let no untruth stand. That must be the job of every American leader who cherishes the course on which this nation was set after the 1960s riots and the Kerner Commission Report which analyzed them.

Racism has endured because the American resolve has been lacking. If this country is to remain competitive into the new century, we must exploit this unique opportunity for reconciliation as we close out the twentieth century and move forward into the twenty-first century. We must talk and "psych" ourselves to a new plateau from which we then will implement racial equality through repetitive, tangible acts. Our future, in a globe of great diversity and color, depends upon it.

Facing an Uncertain Future from Strength

We must approach our tasks with courage and vision, mindful of our past but not shackled by it and unafraid to grasp new ideas appropriate to our present circumstances and dilemmas.

I come today to a place which, second only to the nurturing and enriching cradle of my parents' home, was the fertile launching pad of my flight into my life. North Carolina Central University, called in my youthful time on this campus, simply North Carolina College, was that protected place where I felt and experienced the rare and enviable sensation of being exactly what I was and who I was, without penalty, without prejudice, without qualifying considerations about motives or intentions. North Carolina College was the anvil on which my independent, self assured and assertive character was shaped— legitimizing me into adulthood.

Today we celebrate the vision, the determination, the endurance and the leadership of James E. Shepard, the founding president of North Carolina Central University, whose future is guided by the steady and worldly wise hand of one of its very own sons. Newly inaugurated Chancellor Julius Levonne Chambers, evolved from a past familiar to most of us gathered here, as first, the national religious training school and Chautauqua; then simply the national training school; then Durham State Normal School; then North Carolina College for Negroes. By the time that I arrived, in 1951, this institution had become North Carolina College at Durham, which was the name it retained, until just before my sister Roslyn Scruggs, arrived in 1965, when our institution became North Carolina Central University (NCCU).

Founder's Day is the occasion on which we revisit the odyssey of this institution. It is the official occasion on which, through our revering observances and our words of gratitude, we pay homage to the person to whose efforts we owe this institution's very existence. But today, because I am of this place in a more profound way than even I ever consciously knew, I am given the opportunity of stretching our vicarious knowledge of founder James E. Shepard. Moreover, I am given the chance to acknowledge the manifest destiny of my life's association with this institution, with the State of North Carolina, with President Shepard, with Dr. Alfonso Elder, and with Chancellor Chambers, with all that is this place, in a most personal way. Permit me, therefore, a few moments to weave the magic of this personal story for you, and to "get down and dish", as our young people say, about the real deal involving me and North Carolina.

In 1951, my decision to come to North Carolina College as a student, was as much a decision based upon family ties and background as it was anything else. My father, Leonard Scruggs, was born in Raleigh, North Carolina, on the campus of Shaw University, where his father and my grandfather, Lawson Andrew Scruggs, was a member of Shaw's medical faculty. My grandfather was a unique man, and although he died before I was born, he left us much by way of legacy, history, and the red clay of North Carolina in our souls. A practicing physician and prolific author, Grandfather Scruggs graduated from Shaw University's medical school, also with a degree in literature, in 1887; and, Founder James E. Shepard also graduated from Shaw University.

Grandfather Scruggs then remained at Shaw, as resident physician and instructor in hygiene and physiology, while also serving as resident physician at Leonard Hospital in Raleigh until 1893. As an aside, let me tell you that our family still retains the name "Leonard" in our genealogy—we are now working on Leonard A. Scruggs, IV. During this same period, James E. Shepard, entered Shaw University, in 1890, and graduated in 1894, with a degree in pharmacy.

Now, I don't have to remind us all that in a small black school, before the turn of the century, there were no "sections" of courses from which students were allowed to choose. A student simply took a particular course of study. It was much like the fact that there were no such grades as "I" or "Incomplete" back then. There really weren't any such things as Incompletes when I was a student here in the late 1950s. We all were expected to complete the work. Otherwise, it was understood that we had not completed the work. The value assigned to not completing the work was an "F" not an "I." I can still hear in the ear of my mind, the voice of Caubert Jones and Dr. Farrison, outlining all of the things for which a student could easily earn an "F." And if one needed clarification about the sanctity of this interpretation, one had only to complain to one's parents, who would immediately wonder exactly who was going to pay for the extra time needed to actually "complete" the work which we were supposed to finish during the semester or quarter for which they already paid.

My point is that if one attended Shaw University during the 1890s—when Grandfather Scruggs taught science courses in hygiene and physiology, and you were in the science department, like James E. Shepard was, pursuing, as he was, a degree in pharmacy, you were taught by Dr. Lawson Andrew Scruggs. And so my ties to this place and to this nexus of nurture are deeply rooted in my ancestry and in the history of tangents long since buried.

My choice of NCC instead of Shaw was one of practicality with regard to my chosen field of study, political science, and one of the continuing "in loco parentis" possibilities which my family saw among NCC's faculty: Dr. Helen Edmonds, NCC's revered Professor Emerita of

History and our Chancellor Chambers early mentor, was my mother, Geneva Byrd Scruggs's schoolmate at St. Paul's college in Lawrenceville, Virginia. So my parents, in enabling me to enroll in NCC in many, intentional and inadvertent ways, simply "sent me back home" to the care of extended family and to the nurturing of known values and experiences.

Life is full of such coincidences. It is said that there are no accidents, that everything happens for a reason. So much of those defining life choices which, when I view them retrospectively, had their genesis for me right here on this campus. And the tangents continue. My friend and your chancellor and I have shared dais, dialogues and meetings with the President of the United States. We come, the two of us eagles, out of an ethic, articulated back in 1938 by President James E. Shepard, who observed back then:

> So long as the abundant life is for the Negro an unfulfilled wish, then so long must the Negro element of this great American host lag behind shackled by a racial discrimination, and thus the pace of the whole host of Americans in their onward march of progress be retarded.... We must...remember that the Negro is an integral part of and no program looking toward future betterment and progress can ignore him.

If there is a better context within which to consider, for example, the implications of the North American Free Trade Agreement, or NAFTA, which is being vigorously argued in Washington these days, I have not a clue what it is. But in the arena of higher education these days, other currents are stirring which give pause to those of us produced by institutions like North Carolina Central University, and to which I think that we must pay heed.

It is a new day today. Our population has changed dramatically in this country. Between the census years 1980 and 1990, over 40 percent of the total growth of the American population was the result of immigration. And of that forty-plus percent growth through immigration, over 75 percent was accounted for by Hispanic and Asian immigrants. Of that 75 percent Hispanic and Asian new Americans, about 95 percent settled in and around the largest cities in the United States...those same largest cities in which three out of four black Americans already live, and where 60 percent of all Native Americans live.

With that demographic change has come a new set of imperatives, riveting the attention of African Americans, and focusing that attention on our place, as a group, in American society. Once predominant in numbers and influential among minority groups, and once confident about the life of those institutions which had prepared our leaders— institutions like NCCU, born of larger society fusions of its ethics of separateness and equity, black Americans have been reconsidering some basic assumptions.

One of the major organizations undertaking these reconsiderations has been my own, the Joint Center for Political and Economic Studies, where I direct our Urban Policy Institutes. A national think tank with a special perspective on and toward the black community, the Joint Center recently has issued a seminal study of events in higher education, which have special implications for black Americans. The essay, entitled "The Inclusive University," was prepared by the Joint Center's Committee on Policy for Racial Justice, chaired by historian John Hope Franklin. Other scholars include: James Comer, William Julius Wilson, Roger Wilkins, Drew Days, Sara Lawrence Lightfoot, Mary Frances Berry, Lisle Carter, Jewell Cobb, James Gibbs, and Matthew Holden.

In response to the essay's central question of why the success rate of blacks at Predominantly White Institutions (PWIs) lags woefully behind that of whites, the essay makes this charge: "The fault...lies to a great extent with the institutions themselves." John Hope Franklin's preface sums up this hard-hitting conclusion which, I think, will become part of the future public policy debate on higher education. He says:

> What is required is nothing less than the transformation of our universities into truly inclusive institutions, institutions able to create and maintain an environment that is supportive of all students in search of academic attainment. We do not believe that this is an impossible task, but it will require extraordinary from other segments of the society, including the black community and its leaders. The inclusive university we advocate must not be defined merely by such concepts as multi-culturalism, diversity or openness, all subjects currently being debated inside and outside the academy. For us, the inclusive university must be an institution which accepts the responsibility of providing equal access and opportunity and an accommodating environment for all members of the academic community regardless of racial, ethnic, social or economic background.

"The inclusive university" says the Committee On Policy For Racial Justice, "will be a hospitable, engaging, and supportive place that provides increased opportunities for black students."

> ...[B]ut that is not all that will be achieved. Just as the reforms won by the black-led civil rights movement a generation ago improved life chances for minorities and women, and thus benefited the entire society, so these higher education reform will widen educational opportunities for other historically disadvantaged groups as well as

blacks. To the extent that these purposes are realized, the education levels and productivity of the next generation of adults will be enhanced and the entire society will gain, at home and in its dealings with other nations.

Within this context, our committee focused on a number of issues it considered particularly important. Among these was the concept and policy of affirmative action, as controversial a subject in higher education as in corporate boardrooms and the halls of government. It is a recurring point of contention in education whether one relates it to student admissions and retention, programs to help less prepared individuals succeed, or the recruitment and employment of black faculty and black administrators.

Other controversial issues explored by the committee included 'hate speech' and its dangerous implications for the integrity of colleges and universities and for relationships between blacks and whites; the role of blackhouses on predominantly white campuses and the tendency of black students toward self segregation; and the serious consequences inherent in the exploitation of black athletes by leading universities.

This essay advocates teaching and learning techniques that emphasize cooperation instead of competition and that offer academic assistance to students in need of such help—be it in the form of writing clinics or special mentoring programs. Members of the committee also stress the importance they attach to the presence of black faculty on university campuses in more than token numbers. They consider this to be an essential component of an inclusive university.

The issue of how students raised in poverty or those of modest means can afford to continue their education beyond high school remains one of the major barriers confronting young blacks. Ever increasing fees and major budge problems at every level of government have put higher education into the category of 'luxuries' that many black families simply cannot afford. We struggled to find solutions to this problem, but in the end agreed that it will require the intervention of federal and state governments if students, regardless of color or economic status, are to be given an equal chance to acquire a college education.

...[W]e are convinced that a university that accepts inclusiveness as its mission and modus operandi, will make higher education more accessible and equitable for all and will help define what it means to be an educated man or woman in today's world and in the future.

This essay dares to suggest what kind of university would be most responsive to the needs of our increasingly diverse society and our evermore demanding population. It will no doubt be challenged, cursed, and otherwise put down, but its haunting question will not go away: Why is it that the success rate of blacks lags behind the rates of whites at PWIs and why is it that a conspicuous number of black students are involved in confrontations and other conflict situations on these campuses?

And now a few comments on Historically black Institutions (HBIs) which have played a critical role in the advancement of African Americans and of generations of third world leaders. HBIs also have been, and continue to be, the principle gateway to social and economic advancement for tens of thousands of aspiring young people, and they are still influential centers of creativity and cultural preservation.

Black colleges continue to provide these services, but they do so in an environment of rapid and profound changes that, in many respects, threaten their survival or challenge their reason for being. Some of these changes affect almost all small colleges and universities: declining enrollment, severe financial pressures, and sharp cutbacks in federal government aid for students. But black colleges appear to be more severely affected by these conditions, and they also face some unique pressures which grow out of their own unique history. The viability of many of these educational institutions has long been questioned, and their mission or reasons for being is increasingly being challenged in recent years in the federal courts.

I do not pretend to have a full grasp of these developments or answers for the many dilemmas they pose for black colleges. I will merely attempt here to underscore some aspects of the demographic, economic, and social context in which black colleges are operating today, and suggest some considerations that might help guide our thinking about the future of these institutions.

Even as we note with pride the immensely important contribution black colleges have made and continue to make to blacks and the society at large, it is important to bear in mind, an observation by the late United Negro College Fund Executive William Trent, Jr., that "the Negro Colleges were born in crisis. They have existed on the edge of poverty ever since." Today they are more precariously perched on that edge than at any time in their history, partly because of their small size and their southern locations; partly because of inadequate resources; partly because they serve a higher proportion of needy students requiring financial support and remedial help; and partly because of competition from predominantly white institutions for the best black students and faculty and for the financial resources to support them.

To the best of my knowledge, there is no solution at-hand for this crisis which appears to be headed into the twenty-first century. HBIs face three challenges:

1. **Competition**. To compete effectively in a largely open educational market in spite of the serious handicaps their history imposes. In a society where rigid segregation has all but disappeared, black colleges are compelled to compete with financially stronger, broadly developed institutions to attract both students and faculty. Relatively few black colleges are now equipped to compete successfully with America's leading institutions for the best and the brightest of the black college-bound students or academicians.

2. **Finances**. To adapt their curriculum and educational philosophy to the new needs of blacks and changing needs of the economy. After having invested heavily in the production of teachers for most of their history, HBIs are struggling to meet the need of a new technology-oriented information economy. In recent years we have seen mounting documentation of big performance gaps between black and white students. HBIs need more resources to respond more quickly and aggressively to this disparity.

3. **Adaptation**. To redefine themselves and their mission to adapt to a new environment. black colleges must confront the question of their role in a society no longer committed to the structure of segregation that helped define that role initially. The question gathers urgency especially as we contemplate the future of the public black colleges, which were developed explicitly as alternatives to black inclusion in existing state colleges and universities. Public policy, economic pressures and legal challenges now combine to encourage steps toward mergers or other actions that threaten their existence as black institutions. Moreover,

some observers argue that racially exclusive learning environments could actually handicap blacks who must function in any open society.

I am not among those who doubt that there is a continuing role for black colleges. Nor do I doubt that we are capable of finding and articulating that role in a compelling way. I am convinced, however, that to do so we need to be more creative, critical, flexible, and ingenious than we have been up to now. Without apologies for the past, we need to be willing to contemplate major changes that strengthen the black community and the entire society for the future. We must approach our tasks with courage and vision, mindful of our past but not shackled by it and unafraid to grasp new ideas appropriate to our present circumstances and dilemmas.

For starters, let me suggest four broad notions about how we might proceed:

1. We should shift our emphasis from one of "survival" to building outstanding institutions, competitive in every sense of the word, but still able to respond to the special needs of black youth and the black community. Mere survival in an era of rapid growth and change is hardly a worthy goal. Toward the goal of increased competitiveness, let us be willing to accept fewer institutions, those with the resources and strategic locations that give them the best chances for rapid development as first-rate educational institutions. In doing so, no one need mete out the death sentence to any particular institution. Instead, we can develop rational criteria for the allocation of the limited governmental, philanthropic and other dollar available to support higher education.

2. We should concentrate more on the production of quality graduates

than on ensuring that all who enter our colleges are merely credentialed. To do otherwise is to satisfy an immediate egalitarian urge while consigning black colleges and their students to a life time of rumors of inferiority.

3. We might consider the creative conversion of some black colleges into innovative centers for community education and development that meet some of the numerous new needs of the society, especially black communities, for non-traditional, adult and continuing learning opportunities.

4. In recognition of the larger value of eliminating racial exclusiveness, something for which blacks have worked especially hard, we must be willing to define historically black colleges, not solely as ones with numerical majority of black students, faculty, and administrators, but as institutions that maintain, acknowledge, preserve, and celebrate their place in black and American history, as educational institutions of excellence that pay special attention to the history, needs and aspirations of the black community.

Clearly, these objectives are more easily asserted than achieved. Yet approaches like these appear likely to help move us toward resolving the dilemma of Black colleges by reconciling our commitment to an open educational system on all fronts with the Black community's need for strong institutions that reflect its heritage and respond to its needs. Equally important, this is perhaps the best way to ensure that future generations of African-Americans are genuinely aided by their institutions and not handicapped in the marketplace.

One final thought on how we should approach deliberations and decision on the future of Black colleges. Here, the words of Martin

Luther King, Jr. are instructive. He said:

> It is not a sign of weakness, but a sign of high maturity, to rise to the level of self-criticism. By self-criticism I mean critical thinking about ourselves as a people and the course we have charted or failed to chart.

The future of black colleges may well hinge on our response to this challenge. The future of all institutions of higher education may depend on how we respond to this challenge.

Part Four

Biographies

C. DeLores Tucker: A Lamplighter for the Paths

All of us today—willingly or not—enjoy the benefits of her creative, passionate and dignified determination.

Many years ago, before it was fashionable or revolutionary, C. DeLores Tucker set the standard for political activism in women who looked and acted like ladies and wore soft kid gloves over their iron fists. I remember riding with her on a hot day in the early 1960s, on a rickety ancient elevator in an old office building in Philadelphia. We arrived at the same time to attend the Philadelphia Fellowship Commission's Board of Directors meeting. It was our first time meeting each other. She was an impeccable, gracious and focused matron of thirty-something, already an established leader of good causes and a warrior for equal rights. I was a green, new arrival on that city's social volunteerism scene, a slightly younger wanna-be, just recently appointed to that same board and in awe of her presence as a truly "cool" operator. She exuded poise and confidence. I thought at that moment, and I continue to think to this day: *when I grow up, I want to be like her.*

In the ensuing half-century, she was my patron, I was her collaborator. We became political colleagues, family friends, advocates for African Americans and women of color, and, in the last decade and a half, tenders of the rich legacy of icons from the civil rights movement. Although herself an icon who marched beside Dr. and Mrs. Martin Luther King, Jr., she has remained modest and unselfish. She avoided self-aggrandizement and self-promotion to the extent of literally begging that she not be saluted or given public awards because too many others were more deserving, she said. Yet, hers was the vision and the unrelenting energy that created the National Political Congress of black Women in 1984, institutionalizing the power of black women as professional politicians, and helping to legitimize their demands for places at the electoral table.

In 2002, as a member of the legendary Black Leadership Forum (BLF) which annually honored remarkable leaders in the struggle for civil rights and equality, she extracted a promise that BLF would not only honor her request that she _not_ be cited as a BLF Lamplighter awardee, but also that we not tell her devoted and ardently supportive husband, Bill Tucker, that she had declined to be lauded.

She was deeply humbled by the invitation but was reluctant to be showcased in any way, and she knew that her husband would not agree with her modesty. It was only through my persistence and respect for the person of humility who I knew her to be over all these years that her request finally was granted. It was an unfortunate decision. If ever there was a lamplighter for the paths to equality, justice, and opportunity, it was C. DeLores Tucker.

One of Dr. Tucker's primary delights and pleasures was her work for women who were on the political career ladder and who actively participated in the elective politics. Her stubborn non-partisanship was genuine. Her own career as a political trailblazer sensitized her—she was the first black woman to be elected Secretary of State, (Pennsylvania, 1971–1977); she was the Chair of the Credentials Committee for the Democratic National Convention (1964); and was a Democratic Primary candidate for Congress (Pennsylvania, 1972.) Thus, she deeply appreciated the unique travails of any black woman, of _any_ political persuasion, who had the courage to run for office or to serve as a political appointee.

She created the Commission on Presidential Appointments, which she convened every four years—regardless of who occupied the Oval Office. She personally contacted each President, and through the Commission and her own direct persuasion, promoted a long list of highly qualified black women candidates for one-after-another appointed positions in every single administration since 1984. She was determined to have talented, qualified black women serve in national administrations, and after a few years, she and the Commission promoted several black men as well. She decided that race trumped both gender and party affiliation as the greatest obstacle to the advancement of highly competent African Americans in public office.

Her long illness seems so undeserved. Before she died on October 12, 2005, she had worked hard all of her life—even before the Philadelphia Fellowship Commission—to guarantee equal access and opportunities for all Americans of color and, particularly, for black women. Her peace, at last, is well earned but, personally, I shall truly miss her being in my life. All of us today—willingly or not—enjoy the benefits of her creative, passionate and dignified determination that America live up to its promise of justice and fairness for all, including, as she used to say, its promise to "our African American sisters."

R. Joyce Whitley: Knowing When to Wear White Gloves

Knowing when to wear white gloves, even if you do not choose to wear them, is symbolic of a discipline.

My friend, R. Joyce Whitley, always referred to those of us she counted as friends by a full phrase that sort of ran together: "My friend Yvonne Leftwich" or "my friend Claudia Pharis," or "my friend Anita Burney," or "my friend Arlene," or "my friend Bea Nivens," so that even though we all hadn't really ever seen one another, we really did know one another as Joyce's friends.

My friend Joyce Whitley came from a world of white gloves and tea dances, she both valued and was uncomfortable with these institutions. She often spoke of the specialness of black women like herself—like both of us—who came of age in the 1950s. We were privileged to be able to go to college in a time when such an education was made possible mostly by family and money saved from jobs (sometimes assisted by academic or competitive merit scholarships; almost never with "outside" help like "financial aid" or "student loans"). She thought that this experience, along with our own high expectations of success made us a different breed of black woman. Whitley thought that we were more like our parents before us than like the so-called "modern women" of today. When we talked about these differences – about the pain and sacrifice of growing into womanhood, in spite of being black women, when Joyce reflected on "white-gloved" years at Fisk, and on the words of her college roommate, who said, "Joyce, if we weren't special, we wouldn't even be here!", she would close the train of discourse with a phrase which came to characterize her and my, our, plan for our old age. She would say: "We have to write a book about that!"

Joyce—which I called her without her permission—spent this past election night at my house in Washington, D.C. She called in August to direct me to make an election night party so that she and I, and a few close friends could monitor what we expected to be a sure Clinton victory. She then telephoned a couple of other friends to meet her here. As the evening rolled on, we sounded like fans at a football game. Nothing stimulated her adrenal juices more than the clash in battle about issues and ideas…nothing, except a really good looking man—especially one who was also smart.

Joyce and I met in Washington during the Kennedy and Johnson years. We never lost touch from the first day—thirty years ago—forward until the last Friday of her life. She was an intellectual giant who would call to think out loud about an idea. When the famous writer, Alex Poinsett, heard of her passing last week, he said: "Boy! I remember how she set the graduate school at the University of Chicago on fire when she was a student there!"

She was humble and self effacing, sometimes beating up on herself because she had continued to be gracious and kind to someone who clearly did not deserve such courtesy. And yet, in the final analysis, even when someone "hurt her feelings" (as she described rudeness) she usually opted for "gracious and kind."

Joyce loved the experience which she had as a Rockefeller Fellow at Brown University because it gave her a chance to fulfill a long-standing ambition: to write a play. She said that writing "Dreams of Callahan" was the hardest thing that she ever had to accomplish. But as recently as November, she was giving deep thought to how she might change the ending. She wanted the play to make a stronger statement about black leaders and their neighborhoods and about how public policies foreclose options to those who stand outside of the mainstream.

In writing about her work that evolved into "Dreams of Callahan" Joyce said:

> There was no presumption that my work would be developed into a dramatic form, but there was a presumption that I would develop material that would serve as a base for new truths, new myths reflecting more accurately the reality of Afro-American experience. "Dreams of Callahan" is the result of my thinking about what happened in those black communities with which I worked for so long. I found a more satisfying and accurate way to give voice to my thoughts and my feelings than previously available to me.

We had a series of continuous conversations this year about her play and her mission. It was common for Joyce to open a telephone conversation four or five days after whenever the last conversation had occurred by simply saying, "Yeah! I really should have said that differently." Not, hello. Not, do you remember our conversation about thus and so? She always began in the middle of the action. I tried to be equal to her powerful thought process, but sometimes I failed. She would laugh, which she did easily, at my faltering. She attributed it to my advancing age. She would say, "Yvonne, you're getting old."

And yet for all of the idea talk, for all of the many nights which we spent continuing a day's work of urban planning reports and policy proposal writing; for all of the times we spelled each other by trading visitor lecturer invitations, contracts as "policy advisor" — (she was my consistent intellectual sounding board over the years when I was a deputy mayor or the member of a governor's cabinet, or when I was a HUD Deputy Assistant Secretary, I was her favorite wordsmith), Joyce loved best our late night, hunkered down, unadulterated woman talk. Clothes, shoes, skin treatments, make-up experiments, hair styles, what she called "crisp looks," and men. She had a healthy disregard for food—or at least for having much on hand in her refrigerator. Joyce completely ignored cash money. My task was always to have cash when I met Joyce at the airport or when we went to dinner. She never remembered to go to the bank, but she never forgot her credit cards, so we would exchange. We'd go out to dinner, wherever we were, she'd pay with her cards and I'd give her my part in cash.

Joyce had a philosophy, which I have yet to see bested, about what really counts in this world. She used to tell me that we did not really "get points" for things which we conventionally are taught are the most important:

- Reports need to be erudite—but they also must look good.
- Proposals should be excellent in content—and never late.
- It is fine to give a substantive speech—but one should look the part and should sound impressive—in tone and vocabulary.

One "got points" for knowing what really counts with others and for being sure that we addressed the priorities of those doing the judging— which, in fact, might—and probably did—differ from her ideas, or mine, of what was important.

And Joyce got lots of points. She was creative and observant. She was gracious and complimentary to others in their success. She had a way of linking one person with another, to their mutual benefit. She cared about her family and about her friends. She was generous with her mind—and also with her insight into relationships between men and women. She valued her friends' and family's children, and when tragedy struck—as it inevitably does—she gave of herself to help ease the pain.

Joyce Whitley received a Bachelor of Arts in English from Fisk University, a Master's of Arts in Sociology from Western Reserve University, a Master of Arts in City Planning from University of Chicago, and attended the Harvard University Graduate School of Design.

She was Vice President and Principal in Charge of planning, programming, and space utilization studies with the Shaker Heights firm of Whitley & Whitley Architects and Planners. She was also a 1986–1987 Rockefeller Fellow in the Humanities at Brown University, where she wrote the play, "Dreams of Callahan," staged at Brown University, Karamu House and in Western Pennsylvania. Her playwriting efforts were inspired from her HUD Special Assistant experience in the Carter Administration. Thereafter, she was a State Department delegate in Iran and South Africa at the International Conferences of Architects and Planners. She has authored numerous articles, reports, and papers.

Joyce's many interests and concerns led her to actively serve on the following boards: American Institute of Planners; Board of Governors; Harvard University School of Design; National Board of Directors; Black Economic Union; and Board of Trustees, Karamu House. She was a member of the executive committee, University Circle Incorporated; member of the American Society of Planning Officials; American Planning Association; National Architectural Accreditation Board; Cleveland Planning Commission; visiting committee, Department of Architecture and Planning, Howard University; chairman, community advisory committee to Black Studies Program, Cleveland State University; the NAACP; the Shaker Heights Interest Group; advisory committee, Northeast Ohio Jazz Society; and Fisk University Alumnus

Club. Ms. Whitley has won the Mary McLeod Bethune Award of Merit, the Career Women of Achievement Award, and the Northside Preservation Commission Circle Award and Northside Preservation Commission Award, St. Louis, Missouri.

She liked to go to sleep early in her final years. She hated driving after dark, with good reason. But she loved to lecture to students about the real world—as she did earlier this year at Cornell University, and she loved to find out the real world for herself: she was scheduled to have taken another trip to Africa.

We had been thinking together recently about how women of our era are being over looked in this new day of the "new feminism," how knowing when to carry white gloves, even if you do not choose to wear them, is symbolic of a discipline.

Joyce was, during our last conversation, distilling the experiences of her whole life, in a way designed to yield lessons to younger women—to try to explain how it was for us. As we talked, we both made notes, stopping one another in mid-sentence to say: "Wait a minute! Wait a minute! Say that again! That was good language!"

Our last words together in mid-December were a promise to get to work on an article—or a book—about black women of our age—of great gains and painful losses of being just ten years short of contemporary greatness (as soon as the holidays were over.) When the story is told right, it will trace the life of R. Joyce Whitley—in living color and with bells and whistles.

Byllye Y. Avery: Humanizing the Time in Between

Unify birth and death for black women by humanizing the time which they spend in between these inevitable poles.

For Byllye Yvonne Avery, the incidents among black women of infant mortality and prenatal neglect, of sudden death from hypertension and of premature parenthood from unplanned pregnancy, are statistics which inspired her 1974 co-founding of the Gainesville Women's Health Center. These same concerns led, in 1978, to her founding of BIRTHPLACE, an alternative birthing center also in Gainesville, and five years later in Atlanta, Georgia, led to the incorporation of the internationally renowned National Black Women's Health Project (NBWHP). These innovative and important initiatives, along with twenty years as a selfless activist for responsive, "whole-istic" health care for women, were tangibly acknowledged in 1989 when Avery received a "genius" award of $310,000.00 for individual excellence from the John D. and Catherine T. MacArthur Foundation.

Avery's National Black Women's Health Project (NBWHP) remains headquartered in Atlanta. It has a network of more than 130 groups, twenty-two in the United States and six in foreign countries. Branch offices are located in New York City, Philadelphia, Oakland, and the NBWHP National Public and Education Office is in Washington, D.C. While executive director of NBWHP from 1982–1990, the grassroots advocacy organization swelled to an international network of more than 2,000 black women participants. Although Avery credits three white friends with showing her early on how to navigate institutional systems, NBWHP is still run by black women for black women.

Born in LeLand, Florida in 1937, into the reserved family of a rural teacher, Avery's early life followed a traditional path. Educated as a teacher with a master's degree in special education, her early career years were devoted to teaching special education to emotionally disturbed students and consulting on learning disabilities in public schools and universities throughout the southeastern United States. But when Avery's husband, Wesley, died suddenly of a massive heart attack at age thirty-three, her commitment to whole health care in the black community was born.

As she assumed her single parenthood for her son and daughter, Wesley Jr. and Sonja, Avery also assumed as her responsibility an extended family of black women whom she sought to help end their familiar and painful conditions of extreme stress. Avery initially formed small self-help groups for distressed black women whom she felt were disabled by the poverty which caused their tension, by the crime and violence which often defined their communities and sometimes their homes, and by the raw, oppressive racism which punctuated their daily encounters with the outside world. It was this small group concept that Avery then began to replicate nationally and worldwide.

Avery sought to unify birth and death for black women, by humanizing the time which they spend in between these inevitable poles. Through the self-help groups, within an environment fully supportive of Black women, self-esteem is developed. Moreover, a forum is provided for neutralizing the abusive and negative sexual, health and family experiences of black women.

Avery sees her participation in NBWHP as a lifelong commitment, just as she expects black women's participation and commitment to their "whole-istic" health to be lifelong. So passionate about her cause is Avery that she largely defines herself by NBWHP's accomplishments.

And she refused to stop there, Avery's activist-spirit compelled her to sponsor the First National Conference on Black Women's Health Issues; develop the first Center for Black Women's Wellness; produce "On Becoming a Woman: Mothers and Daughters Talking to Each Other" the first ever documentary film that explores sexuality and reproduction from their perspective; pioneer the Avoidable Mortality Cancer Project jointly with Morehouse School of Medicine and The National Center for Teen Parents in Bennettsville, South Carolina; and form the Florida Healthy Mothers / Healthy Babies Coalition.

Avery has served as a board member of The New World Foundation; The Global Fund for Women; International Women's Health Coalition; Boston Women's Health Book Collective, and, the Advisory Committee for the Kellogg International Fellowship Program. Recognized as a dreamer, visionary and grassroots realist, Byllye Avery, L.H.D., is a member of the LLuminari network of experts, and founder of The Avery Institute for Social Change, and the Black Women's Health Imperative (formerly the National Black Women's Health Project.) She recently won Lifetime Television's "Trailblazer Award" and the *Essence* magazine award for community service. Avery lives out her understanding of sisterhood by being both blood-kin and / or friend-kin to the women whose lives she's touched.

Florence May Rice: Change Agent Extraordinaire

"I was coming in for the benefit of my community. When you are representing your community, you never want to do anything to disgrace them."

—*Florence M. Rice*

Florence May Rice usually leaves her apartment in upper-central Harlem shortly after eight o'clock each morning. She does not leave before eight because long distance telephone rates are cheapest at that time of day. So that is when she makes her long-distance calls to fellow consumer advocates around the country. And if anyone in the world knows when and where the consumer can get the best buy from the telephone company—or from any other utility for that matter, it is Florence May Rice.

It was because of her watchdogging, the giant utilities on behalf of the poor and minorities, *THE NATION* magazine christened her "Harlem's Nader Raider" in 1971. Rice responded: "There are not enough Ralph Naders and there are not enough Florence Rices." She conservatively estimates that she has been fighting the establishment for sixty of her seventy-three years.

"A perpetually angry, one-woman consumer movement" she is a champion of the underdog—and especially the black underdog—because she considers herself one. Her initiation into the ranks of advocacy came through her association with unions, initially with the ILGWU in 1962 when she worked in the garment district of New York City.

In a 1977 *New York Times* article Rice stated:

> It all started in the 1960s when I was working for a children's outerwear company. I was a "chairlady" (for the Union) in charge of the black folks. You know, it becomes very vivid in your mind You have to be aware that you're just there as a token—as a hammer over the head of the Black folks and to keep your foot up the black folk's butts but you can do nothing with the white folks. And you begin to identify that because you see what's happening.... And that is what caused me to turn around—to turn against the union, and ....To realize Negroes—or blacks, or African-Americans or whatever anyone wants to call us....We are the victims everywhere of racism. I came to see how deep-seated racism was...whether it was in the unions or where we were spending our dollars—everywhere....

It was then that Rice, much against her will, began to act on the courage of a growing conviction that she had to speak up for her rights as well as other people's, or no one else would. The United States House of Representatives was in the midst of the infamous investigation of trade unions. A *New York Post* article about improprieties and sweetheart contracts cites her as a primary government witness. She charged the unions with "...racial discrimination...against Negro and Puerto Rican workers" and with trying "...to intimidate witnesses, threatening penalties if they appear at the hearings in the U.S. Court House."

Citing this single incident as her baptism by fire of advocacy, Rice reflects:

> I never wanted to be out there, to be a leader, I'm a follower. But at the hearing everyone started to drop out like flies, because they didn't want to jeopardize their jobs. So I made up my mind that somebody

had to do it and I came forward. I knew that by doing it I was putting a rope around my own neck. But I did it anyway. And the union blackballed me for years. I couldn't get any job anywhere until finally a fellow maverick found a job for me on 125th Street, the heart of Harlem.

Rice says that her then-mentor, a man, talked her into picketing the union as her first act of civil disobedience.

"He took me out [of the sweatshop], threw me in the ocean, and said: 'Now, swim!'"

Recalling how this early experience prepared her for her direct confrontations with the giant utilities, she speaks of her first meeting with executives of the telephone company:

When I got to the downtown Manhattan address, the woman who was to meet me was nowhere in sight. So I went on up to the conference room alone. When I got upstairs and I walked in the room, those utility telephone people were standing there. The way that they looked at me, it was like they thought that I had to be the cleaning woman. Over the years, I've stayed in that room and gained the respect of those men.

How?

I don't get familiar with those people and I never played the sex game. I was coming in for the benefit of my community. When you are representing your community, you never want to do anything to disgrace them. Also, when I was a young woman, white men always assumed that they could get any black woman that they saw. I can truthfully say that I never played that game.

Preparation for life's work takes many forms. In the case of Rice, the training was in the school of hard knocks. Some of the instructors were various operatives within the child welfare network: foster parents, both good and bad; welfare workers, both well meaning and misguided; and a birth mother, over-burdened with six other children.

Several years after her birth in 1919, young Rice began her odyssey among many foster homes. First, she was a resident in the New York Nursery and Child Home, and later, until 1929, in the Colored Orphan Asylum at Riverdale, New York City. Regardless of whether her current foster was in Queens, Peekskill, Sparkville, the Lower East Side, or Brooklyn—all of a few of the sites where she lived—Rice always went to school. "I was blessed in that way. When you were in foster care, you had to go to school."

But when she was thirteen years old, and only in her first year of high school, she ran away from a difficult relationship with her reappeared mother, and from school. She says now that her mother inadvertently became a primary motivator for her life as an activist and change agent: "I knew that I didn't want to be my mother."

Although Rice never completed traditional high school, she has undertaken continuing education constantly since she reached her thirties; typing at the Henry George School, World Affairs at the Walton School, and courses in banking. This year she heard a professor lecture on the effects of "images" on shoppers' preferences and individuals' evaluations of themselves. She intends to enroll in this professor's course next autumn.

Married once when she was very young for a very brief period, "a hot minute! I get an 'F' for picking men!" Her proudest accomplishment is her family. She credits their stability with allowing her the freedom to afford her destiny as an impoverished activist.

> My daughter had the good sense to pick a good husband. They, along with my two grandchildren and my four great-grandchildren, have given me such pride and satisfaction. Also, when I was a young woman, I had the privilege of hooking up with a woman who welcomed me as a member of the Council of Volunteers for the Red Shield. She valued the few skills which I did have and dragged me along to meetings and conferences everywhere. I was so impressed with her involvement in so many causes, I tried to be like her. She helped me to gain my confidence in myself. I try to never forget those people who helped me over the bridge.

Five feet tall, compactly built, Rice carries two items with her at all times. One is an oversized purse, stocked to accommodate her regular daily schedule of community meetings and visits with exploited inner-city residents to hear their complaints and to advise them about their rights. The other item varies in external appearance but never in contents, it is a tote bag or briefcase; a utility bag or large envelope; a container of some description to hold her papers. She has letters from the President about her most recent national consumer award. There are draft program materials from her annual Consumers Conference, at which the White House advisor on Consumer Affairs usually is the keynote speaker. There are regular reports from Comptroller of the currency on banking practices in the inner city; a newsletter put out by Harlem Consumer Education Council, of which she is the founder and president.

Frequently she learns via her community "grapevine" or from one of her confederates within the utilities' bureaucracy of public hearings and press conferences which the utilities have scheduled without giving her notice. Sometimes a crisis or an issue surfaces during the course of the day. She easily gains radio or educational television time to respond. Thus, among her normal paper-load are copies of a one-page biographical sketch which she has available for such unscheduled speeches and statements:

> Born in Buffalo, New York, reared in orphanages and foster homes, Florence M. Rice knows what it means to be alone. Her efforts on behalf of the Harlem Consumers, exploited by dishonest merchants, have removed them from a feeling of isolation and helplessness, making them aware of their rights, and confident of obtaining redress.

This is how she sees herself. I have not heard her better described. When she talks about her life, she often mentions that she does not have any money and never has expected to have any. She ruminates, half in jest, that it would be nice to get cash once in a while when she gets the plaques and certificates.

She worries that there are no young people whom she can groom to take over after she is gone. She is unhappy that she has been unable to get blacks to understand the importance of the Federal Reserve System and its policies. Her Consumers Conference last year focused on the invasion of privacy by various telecommunications gadgets and so-called smart technology. In Rice's view, these innovations are fine for middle-class people with money who know how to protect themselves from electronic snooping.

> But poor blacks and Puerto Ricans won't know what hit us. It is not good that telephone numbers can be monitored by the person who

has been called. It is just another form of redlining. After all, if a merchant or a retailer doesn't want to sell to us or provide service to us, all he has to do is to look at the incoming caller's telephone number. We live in ghettos still and we still have ghetto telephone numbers. Everybody knows that.

She has volumes of newspaper clippings vindicating her assaults against the New York telephone company "Florence Rice Fights the Phone Company—Unpaid" or against utilities in general, "Florence Rice vs. The Utilities" or against usurious retailers, "Furniture Store Accused of Fraud."

Florence May Rice, change agent extraordinaire, is the recipient of the Urban League's Frederick Douglass Medallion; of the OWL Award from the National Older Women's League; and President Bush's Letter of Commendation. She was a member of the Consumer Advisory Council of the Federal Reserve System for three years; and a participant in the first White House Conference on Minority Consumer Issues. In tribute to her half-century of contributions, she was awarded a lifetime membership in the National Consumers Union. She has earned distinction.

"Life is what you make it. You make the decision. You stand the crossroad. You can go left, or you can go right, but no one can ever make you do anything. It helps people not to be bitter. Sympathy is never wasted except when you give it to yourself."

Julia Outterbridge-Robinson: Changing the Complexion of the Mainstream

"I got involved as a fair housing volunteer because I was just so amazed at white folks going to the lengths that this group did to be supportive of blacks…. We worked together as scouts, and later, as 'Test Teams,' finding vacant houses in suburban neighborhoods for minorities to buy. Realtors wouldn't list, and tried to hide these houses, as a way of keeping minorities out of the communities."

—*Julia Outterbridge-Robinson*

Although she never went to undergraduate school to get a bachelor's degree, Julia Outterbridge-Robinson was accepted into the University of Pennsylvania's graduate school and earned a master's degree in city and regional planning. Although her parents strongly discouraged her academic aspirations—telling her what she couldn't do and where the boundaries were that she shouldn't cross—she became the first black valedictorian ever in her high school. She was one on of the first three blacks ever hired by a Philadelphia bank in a white-collar position. She got this job when she was a seventeen-year-old high school graduate.

> When I graduated from high school in 1953, and finally began to recover from the disappointment of not being able to go to college, I picked up the 'Want Ad' section of the newspaper one Sunday. And, given my style, I just walked in and presented myself at Pennsylvania Bank, at an insurance company, and at the telephone company. I said that I wanted a job. After they had advertised the vacancies, I just believed that they meant everybody. They tested me that same day.

> A few days later, my high school guidance counselor, who had been

very supportive, called me to give me advice about which of the jobs I should accept. In those days she was quite unusual because most white counselors tried to dissuade blacks from following their aspirations for college. She knew my family situation and that there was no money for college, so she advised me to accept the bank's job offer. She even already had given me a strong recommendation when they called her for a reference. And lo and behold, they hired me, much to the chagrin of my mother, particularly, who thought that I was brazen and out of place and would end up getting serious problems because of my forward behavior.

That's why I became an activist. It was in rebellion against what I saw around me. I was upset and angry because people around me obviously were not getting an education, housing, or the jobs which they deserved and they were suffering. Yet, they seemed to me to be resigned to their fate. All throughout my early life I was told, what I couldn't do, what I had better not do, that it was all useless. Without once seeing them do anything to change the conditions.

I became very determined not to have my life follow that same course. I knew that I wanted my children to know that there is a big, bad world out there that needed changing and that they could do something to make it a better place. And while I was very angry with my family, I came to realize that they had been trying to protect me from what they saw as ultimate hurt and disappointment.

Robinson, at fifty-five years of age is articulate and clear about her activism. Since that first barrier-breaching at the Pennsylvania Bank— she actually continued to work there in many different capacities for thirteen years—she has devoted her life to changing the "complexion" of mainstream institutions. Her work as a volunteer, as paid staff, has almost always been with organizations devoted to increasing the number of blacks who gain access to society's benefits. Moreover, Robinson and her husband have lived their beliefs on a personal level. Robinson married her childhood sweetheart when she was eighteen, and he was twenty-three and in the Air Force. When he finished his G.I. Bill sponsored master's degree, the housing integration movement, led by their pastor, Reverend Leon Sullivan, was gaining momentum. Her family was looking for a house to buy. Robinson remembers being excited by the prospect of them being one of the black test families who would collaborate with white test agents in opening the suburban communities to blacks who wanted to buy homes.

> The thing that turned my life around was volunteer work in the Civil Rights Movement, and in fair housing when we decided to look for a house. We were the first "test couple" for a suburban integrationist group seeking open housing on Philadelphia's Main Line [a cluster of old and historically exclusive townships surrounding the city.]

> I got involved as a fair housing volunteer because I was just so amazed by what I saw. I had never had the experience of seeing white folks going to the lengths that this group did to be supportive of blacks. After we moved into King of Prussia, it was just unbelievable how supportive they continued to be. So I decided that these were the kinds of people I wanted to spend time with.

Robinson has worked for the American Friends Service Committee, an organization of the Quaker sect, which is renowned for espousing the cause of the disenfranchised and oppressed, both here and abroad. Later, as a result of relationships cemented there, she was employed by the Philadelphia Housing Association, a prestigious housing-quality watchdog organization. She has worked as a community organizer for a depressed, predominantly black neighborhood in south Philadelphia, assisting them in planning to counter an inevitable tide of gentrification. Robinson has also experienced the process of bringing about institutional change from within. As a member of the Mayor's Cabinet, she served as Philadelphia's Housing Director and in several other public service capacities with City and Pennsylvania state government. She was born in North Philadelphia and has always lived in some part of the Philadelphia region.

When Robinson entered the University of Pennsylvania in 1971, she presented herself with a major challenge. Based upon years of "experimental learning" and validated by "fairly decent" LSAT scores, she effectively skipped college and went directly into graduate school full-time. At that same time she also was a wife and mother of three children—all still at home and young. Nonetheless, Robinson completed the two-year program successfully and on time, in spite of a personal tragedy; during the final semester of her second year, her youngest child, a four-year-old daughter, was seriously burned in a fire. Robinson explains:

> I attribute my drive to the encouragement which I received from people in my life who were role models for me. An eighth grade algebra teacher, named Connie Pierce, who died recently was probably the most influential person in my life. A young black woman, she was the one who set the tone for me and gave me a lot of the aspirations for my life. In fact, when I began wanting to go to college, it was because she was a teacher and I admired her so.

> I had never known anyone who had gone to college among my neighbors, parents, or friends. Even my brothers and sisters—of whom there were nine in addition to me—did not go to college, any of them.

But even earlier, before I met Connie Pierce, I wanted to be a lawyer. Don's ask me why. I had never known a lawyer in my life personally, and we didn't have T.V. role models in those days because we didn't have television. But I wanted either to be a teacher like Connie Pierce, or a lawyer ... like nobody I'd ever known.

Although we did better than many families in our neighborhood, we owned our house, the idea of going to college was foreign, everywhere around me, except with Mrs. Pierce and in my dreams. So I made it happen later in my life.

Many who know Robinson find her remarkable. In addition to her relaxed presence at the ramparts of change, the neat, compact, emotionally balanced woman has carried personal burdens heavier than can ever be imagined. The young daughter who recovered from the fire injuries, was involved in an automobile accident fifteen years later, seriously injuring her ankle. The Robinson's middle son, Steven, who as a teenager of great charm and promise was profoundly injured in an automobile accident by a drunken driver, made a remarkable and essentially complete recovery. Yet, without warning, six years later, when he was in college getting on with his life, he died in his sleep from the lingering effects of his ordeal.

Robinson says that she has accepted these burdens with much more peace and understanding than other people really imagine. The Robinson's oldest son is college educated and a successful professional. Their daughter returned to college and graduated in 1991.

I have a very strong faith, and a deep belief that my life has been as it was intended to be and has been more fulfilling than life is for many others. I have seen my mission as striving to learn and to bring other people along with me as I have progressed.

I have been blessed in my marriage and lifelong friendship with my husband. I have been able to make a difference in my life and in the lives of others, and I know deep inside that because of some of my efforts and the efforts of those who have worked along with me—black and white—some injustices which we fought will never exist in that form again.

Susan Deniece Stukes, D.D.S.: The Hard Sciences

"I'm grateful. I want to give back in appreciation for what I have, including my own health."

—*Susan D. Stukes*

She was a twenty-six-year-old captain in the Dental Corps of the United States Army in 1985. Stationed at Fort Polk, Louisiana, Dr. Susan Deniece Stukes was just beginning her journey away from the cushioned middle-class comfort of suburban New York's Westchester County. She says that her three years with the Army in the rural southern community was the genesis of her commitment to changing lives—her own as well as others.

> I look at the people around me in the prison where I have clinic: very young and very sick. I feel that I have been blessed with all that I have for a reason. I could have been born into poverty and ended up in prison, without opportunities. I could have been born sick. But I wasn't. It makes me think about why I'm really here.

Born into privilege and the expectations of accomplishment, her father is a certified public accountant with his own well-established firm; her mother is a teacher, Dr. Stukes has broken from the mold that her background seemed to predetermine. Although she was trained in a solidly middle-class tradition—college at Ohio State University, dental school at Howard University—she has chosen a path of exceptional activism with precise deliberation. And, from that series of choices, she has emerged as a dynamic young change agent, dedicated to the welfare of poor and deprived people in many "third world type" communities, including the rural south U.S.A.

I think I've always been one who just sort of does things rather than to sit and talk about doing things. After I think about something that needs to be changed, I just find a way to do it.

As a high school student, not yet clear that dentistry was her career choice, Stukes was:

...[I]nvolved in everything. Even when I got to college, I continued in student government, where I was the Director of Minority Affairs. I even worked in a local political campaign in Columbus, Ohio, for a congressional candidate, and I worked in voter registration. I wanted to be everything from a veterinarian, to a teacher, to a volunteer with the Peace Corps! Anything interesting that came along, I wanted to do.

Deciding on dentistry while in college was almost a self-fulfilling prophesy. She has always been attracted to the hard sciences and in spite of a brief flirtation with accounting (her father's influence) her focus increasingly narrowed to dentistry. Predestination, she feels, caused her undergraduate Ohio State faculty advisor to be a black dentist who gave her positive encouragement. Stukes graduated from dental school in 1985.

Originally, I planned to open a private practice like everyone else. But as I neared graduation, I began to question the value for me of a traditional residency, and saw the Army as offering an attractive alternative. I could use the three-year tour of duty to polish my skills and to explore what I really wanted to do. Also the Army paid more, had better hours and offered better benefits. The choice changed my life.

I was stationed at Fort Polk, in Leesville, Louisiana. This alone changed the way that I looked at things around me. I learned to accept people for what and who they are, and I learned that there is more to life than material thing, a big house, a nice car. A lot of the people around me, I lived off base and made friends with the local people, didn't have a lot of money but they made a good living off the land and they were at peace.

Civilian life quickly demanded that Dr. Stukes once again stretch into new arenas. Reluctantly starting a private practice in White Plains, New York, she also began advanced training in public health. It is this field which has given this creative young woman entre to her role as an activist health professional. She closed her practice after three years in order to accept a job as a dentist in the New York State prison system.

I have been working in the prison for two years, every day, with both men and women. This experience raised my appreciation of my own good fortune to a new level. When I was in the Army, I was working essentially around well people, because if you were a sick person, the Army would put you out! I look at the people around me in the prison where I have clinic, they have every disease known to man, especially the women. Many can't read and can't write at all.

Seeing that something needs to be done makes me want to do my share and contribute as much as I can. Now, I want to get other people to feel that way also. That's the reason that I and the people in my group want to let other people know what we're doing. Maybe, even if they don't want to get involved with what we are doing, they will be encouraged to get their own group together to do something else to help.

What Stukes is "doing" is founding, organizing, and being president of an international organization which is literally carrying healthcare to hundreds of people in Haiti, Jamaica, the Cameroon, Mali and Guinea, but also to Native Americans in Baton Rouge, Louisiana. The commitment to the welfare of others, which had begun in Louisiana near an Army barracks, is finding new expression in Lascohobas, Haiti. The International Health Professions Network (IHPN) will assign over sixty doctors, plus an undetermined but growing number of technicians, nurses and assistants, to preventive health and dentistry teams and fact-finding missions. They will make trips, carrying all of their equipment, medicines, and treatment supplies to the third world countries on Stukes's list.

On her first trip, before the beginning of IHPN, there were ten health professionals, including Stukes, who went to Lascohobas, Haiti. The Links, Inc., a black women's social service organization provided funding for Project Smile, an organization that distributes toothbrushes, gives dental hygiene classes, cleans teeth and applies fluoride treatments. A member herself, Stukes thought that The Links probably would only be interested in buying the supplies or contributing toward the expenses. Instead, her enthusiasm was so infectious that the organization paid for everything, including the cost of her transportation and maintenance for the ten-day visit.

> It was one of those things in which you can see how the vents in your life sort of fall into place. In the Army, I had learned how to set up mobile dental clinics in the forest, and how to use portable units anywhere. I don't even have to have a foundation. So going to Haiti seemed like it was my destiny waiting for me to come along.

> The experience completely changed my mind about everything. When I came back from Haiti, I looked at things very differently, with more patience and compassion. Just seeing how little people had, put everything into perspective for me and made little daily problems seem

174

insignificant by comparison. In Haiti, if you get sick, it's a least a three hour ride to the doctor, that is even if you can afford to see a doctor. I'm grateful. I want to give back in appreciation for what I have, including my own health.

During her Project Smile maiden venture, the dentist treated 150 Haitian children. She now makes regular follow-up visits every six months, often with newly recruited medical personnel, offering additional specialties. Meanwhile, Stukes is learning French gradually. Her priorities are quite pragmatic.

Last year I learned to say, please sit down. This year, I learned, please leave. The need is so great that there are people everywhere, all over the place.

Now affiliated with the well-known Phelps Stokes Fund, and incorporated with officers who are fellow dentists, Stukes is looking to expand IHPN's services. In Jamaica, where the group also has repetitive visits, the prospect of taking over one of the empty clinics that exist in the Jamaican mountains is the most current endeavor. To be staffed by a nursing staff and dental nurses who have been trained by Stukes and her team, the clinic will become another outpost of her activist network.

Responding to a request from a former classmate who practices dentistry in the Cameroon, a team will visit that country in 1990. Later, with an expanded capacity IHPN will try to establish a birthing center in one of the African countries.

In the final analysis, when I look back, I realize that much of my life also has been influenced by the women in my own family. My mother and my aunt both are strong women with a sense of duty and purpose. When I was growing up, I used to listen to their AKA (Alpha Kappa

Alpha sorority) meetings, and watch how they all carried themselves. Even now, the women with whom I'm associated are strong examples. They don't sit around, they go after their objectives.

About the Author

With more than a hundred publications to her credit, Dr. Yvonne Scruggs-Leftwich writes about issues germane to women, African Americans, other minorities, and union workers. Her areas of expertise include urban policy, politics, public administration and governmental affairs; civil rights; women's issues; labor education and grassroots activism; city and regional planning; strategic planning; and leadership theory.

For more than four decades, Dr. Scruggs-Leftwich has worked as a government official, professor, policy analyst, community activist, author, and spokesperson. She served, for a decade, as executive director and chief operating officer of the national Black Leadership Forum, Inc., the premier coalition of leaders of the top African American civil rights and service organizations. Currently, she also teaches at the National Labor College, George Meany Campus in the Washington, D.C. area

Dr. Scruggs-Leftwich holds a Ph.D. from the University of Pennsylvania; a master's degree from the University of Minnesota's Hubert H. Humphrey School of Public Affairs; a bachelor's degree with honors from North Carolina Central University; and, she was a Fulbright Fellow to Germany.

Previously, she was the Deputy Mayor of Philadelphia, Pa.; New York State's Housing Commissioner; Deputy Assistant Secretary, U.S. Department of Housing and Urban Development (HUD); Executive Director of President Jimmy Carter's Urban and Regional Policy Group which issued the nation's first National Urban Policy; and Director of the Urban and National Policy Institutes for the Joint Center for Political

177

and Economic Studies, among other positions. Dr. Scruggs-Leftwich also has co-owned, with her husband, Reverend Edward V. Leftwich, several non-depository banking corporations, and served as a Consulting Vice-president in the municipal finance field.

She is the mother of four adults—three daughters and a son. Also, the Leftwichs are the grandparents of three young boys.

Hold Fast Your Dreams

Hold fast your dreams!
Let not fate nor loss nor misery
Shatter your castles of hope.
Let not the glimmer of wealth and fame
Tear down your standards of noble living—
For nobility limits not itself to spheres of wealth
      And fame.

Hold fast your dreams!
Build ye stately mansions of strength
      And courage
Climb the high mountains of morality
And reach high up to the peaks of dignity and grace.
Swim wide in the oceans of knowledge
And garner for yourself rich stores of
      Literary Beauty—
For knowledge, morality, strength, courage and beauty
Belong to all who would grasp them.

Hold fast your dreams!
Dream of the future of which you will be a part—
For dreams project you into that cast unknown.
Search.
Search for those things that add richness to your life
And depth to your living—
For life is fullest when richness and depth
Are found in searching.

Hold fast your dreams!
Dreams of peace, of love, of service, and of truth.
Dreams of children remembering the simple things
That make childhood wonderful—
Dreams of violets in the spring,
Roses in summer and acorns in the fall,
Dreams of frost and snow, ice and sleet
And high winds whistling through the trees.
Dream!
Dream of sun and showers,
Blue skies at noonday,
Awaking dawn and shadowy dusk.
Dream of all the joys of nature—
For nature holds not itself from anyone.

Hold fast your dreams!!!
And through your dreams reach heavenward
And touch the hand of God!

                          —Geneva B. Scruggs, 1964

Family Photos

Family Photo Identification List

Page 180 (L–R):

Daughter Cathryn D. Perry; brother Leonard A. Scruggs, Jr.; son-in-law Mitchell R. Glickstein; son Edward V. Leftwich, III; grandson Hunter Perry Glickstein; YSL; husband Rev. Edward V. Leftwich, Jr.; daughter Geneva-Rebecca Perry Glickstein; daughter Tienne D. Leftwich Davis; (Seated) god daughter Tavia F. Evans; and sister Harriet A. Scruggs.

Daughters Lisa Torres; Rebecca Perry Glickstein; Cathryn D. Perry; Tienne Leftwich Davis; Hunter Perry Glickstein; and dad/grandfather Ed.

Daughter Tienne and YSL.

Cousin Dr. Ann Y. Bynum; brother Leonard (kneeling); Mother's sister and our Matriarch Aunt Anna—Dr. Anna Byrd Wheaton; cousin Barbara Smith Rhodes; YSL; and cousin-in-law, the late Tim Rhodes.

Tienne Leftwich Davis with sons, Avery Davis and James Edward Horn.

The Leftwichs.

(Center) The Scruggs Kids: Harriet Scruggs; Roslyn E. Scruggs; Leonard A. Scruggs, Jr.; and YSL.

Granny/god mother and dear sister-friend, Dr. Sally A. Ross with her "children": Cathryn Perry; Rebecca Perry Glickstein; and god son (YSL's grandson) Hunter Perry Glickstein.

Page 181 (L–R):

YSL with son Jason (i.e. Edward V. Leftwich III)

Cathryn, YSL, and Rebecca.

Tienne, YSL, and sister Harriet Scruggs.

YSL with grandsons, Avery and James.

YSL's daughter, Rebecca; Dr. Ross; Megan Pulliam; and daughter Cathryn.

Sister-friend Lee Bickers Perrin and YSL.

Appendix

Bibliography
Organizations
Index

Bibliography

Baldwin, James. 1965. *Notes of a Native Son*. Boston: Beacon Press.

—. 1963. *The Fire Next Time*. New York: Dial Press.

Bell, Derrick A. 1994. *Confronting Authority Reflections of an Ardent Protester*. Boston: Beacon Press.

—. 1992. *Faces at the Bottom of the Well: The Permanence of Racism*. New York, NY: Basic Books.

Bernard, Jessie. 1971. *Women and The Public Interest; An Essay on Policy and Protest*. Chicago: Aldine · Atherton.

Boas, Franz. 1963. *The Mind of The Primitive Man*. London: Collier.

Babson, Steve. 1999. *The Unfinished Struggle Turning Points in American Labor, 1877-Present*. Critical issues in history. Lanham, Md: Rowman & Littlefield.

Bennett, Lerone. 1979. *Wade in The Water: Great Moments in Black History*. Chicago, Ill., USA: Johnson Pub. Co.

Brown, Elaine. 1992. *A Taste of Power A Black Woman's Story*. New York: Pantheon Books.

Brooks, Gwendolyn. 1987. *Blacks*. Chicago: Third World Press.

Comer, James P. 1997. *Waiting for a Miracle: Why Schools Can't Solve Our Problems—And How We Can*. New York, N.Y., U.S.A.: Dutton.

Curtis, Alan. 2004. *Patriotism, Democracy, and Common Sense Restoring America's Promise at Home and Abroad*. [Washington, D.C.]: Milton S. Eisenhower Foundation.

Dante Alighieri, Lawrence Grant White, and Gustave Doré. 1948. *The*

Divine Comedy: The Inferno, Purgatorio, and Paradiso. New York: Pantheon Books.

Douglass, Frederick. 1968. *My Bondage and My Freedom*. The American Negro, his history and literature. New York: Arno Press.

Driskell, David C., David L. Lewis, and Deborah Willis. 1987. *Harlem Renaissance: Art of Black America*. New York: The Studio Museum in Harlem.

D'Souza, Dinesh. 1995. *The End of Racism: Principles for a Multiracial Society*. New York: Free Press.

Edelman, Marian Wright. 1992. *The Measure of Our Success A Letter to My Children and Ours*. Boston: Beacon Press.

Franklin, John Hope. 2005. *Mirror to America: The Autobiography of John Hope Franklin*. New York: Farrar, Straus and Giroux.

—.1976. *Racial Equality in America*. Jefferson lecture in the humanities, 1976. Chicago: University of Chicago Press.

—. 1976. *Racial Equality in America*. Jefferson lecture in the humanities, 1976. Chicago: University of Chicago Press.

—. 1967. *From Slavery to Freedom: A History of Negro Americans*. New York: Knopf.

Gates, Henry Louis, and Anthony Appiah. 1993. *Gloria Naylor Critical Perspectives Past and Present*. Amistad Literary Series. New York: Amistad.

Gibbs, Jewelle Taylor. 1999. "The California Crucible: Towards a New Paradigm of Race and

—. 1996. *Race And Justice: Rodney King and O.J. Simpson in a House*

Divided. San Francisco: Jossey-Bass. Ethnic Relations". *Journal of Multicultural Social Work*. 7 (1–2): 1–18.

Hacker, Andrew. 1992. *Two Nations: Black and White, Separate, Hostile, Unequal*. New York: Scribner's.

Harris, Fred R., and Lynn A. Curtis. 1998. *Locked in The Poorhouse Cities, Race, and Poverty in The United States*. Lanham: Rowman & Littlefield.

Heagerty, Leo E. 1993. *Eyes on the President George Bush: History in Essays & Cartoons*. Occidental, CA: Chronos Pub.

Height, Dorothy I. 2003. *Open Wide the Freedom Gates A Memoir*. New York: Public Affairs.

Herring, Cedric. 1997. *African Americans and the Public Agenda the Paradoxes of Public Policy*. Thousand Oaks, Calif: Sage Publications.

Herrnstein, Richard J., and Charles A. Murray. 1994. *The Bell Curve: Intelligence and Class Structure in American Life*. New York: Free Press.

Higginbotham, A Leon. 1996. *Shades of Freedom: Racial Politics and Presumptions of the American Legal Process*. New York: Oxford University Press.

—. 1980. *In The Matter of Color Race and the American Legal Process: The Colonial Period*. Oxford [etc.]: Oxford University Press.

Hill, Herbert, and James E. Jones. 1993. *Race In America: The Struggle for Equality*. Madison, Wis: University of Wisconsin Press.

Holden, Matthew. 1994. *The Challenge to Racial Stratification*. National Political Science Review, v. 4. New Brunswick, N.J.: Transaction Publishers.

hooks, bell. 2000. *Where We Stand Class Matters*. New York: Routledge.

—.1995. *Killing Rage: Ending Racism*. New York: H. Holt and Co.

—. 1993. *Sisters of the Yam Black Women and Self-recovery*. Boston, MA: South End Press.

Jordan, June. 2002. *Some of Us Did Not Die New and Selected Essays of June Jordan*. New York: Basic/Civitas Books.

—. 1985. *Living Room: New Poems*. New York: Thunder's Mouth Press.

—. 1985. *On Call: Political Essays*. Boston, MA: South End Press.

Jordan, Vernon E., and Annette Gordon-Reed. 2001. *Vernon Can Read! A Memoir*. New York: Public Affairs.

Lawrence-Lightfoot, Sara. 1994. *I've Known Rivers Lives of Loss and Liberation*. Reading, Mass: Addison-Wesley Pub.

Lewis, David L. 1988. *The Race to Fashoda European Colonialism and African Resistance in the Scramble for Africa*. New York: Weidenfeld & Nicolson.

—. 1978. *King: A Biography*. Blacks in the New World. Urbana: University of Illinois Press.

Locke, Alain LeRoy, and Jeffrey C. Stewart. 1992. *Race Contacts and Interracial Relations: Lectures on the Theory and Practice of Race*. Moorland-Spingarn series. Washington, D.C.: Howard University Press.

Madhubuti, Haki R. 1978. *Enemies: The Clash of Races*. Chicago: Third World Press.

Marable, Manning. 2002. *The Great Wells of Democracy: The Meaning of Race in American Life*. New York: Basic Books.

Moynihan, Daniel P. 1970. *Toward A National Urban Policy*. New York: Basic Books.

National Black Women's Health Project. 1987. *On Becoming a Woman Mothers & Daughters Talking Together: A Film.* New York, N.Y.: Distributed by Women Make Movies.

National Council of Negro Women. 1996. *Voices of Vision African American Women on The Issues.* [Washington, D.C.]: National Council of Negro Women.

Quindlen, Anna. 2004. *Loud and Clear.* New York: Random House.

Robinson, Randall. 2000. *The Debt What America Owes to Blacks.* New York: Dutton.

—. 1998. *Defending The Spirit a Black Life in America.* New York, N.Y., U.S.A.: Dutton.

Rowan, Carl T. 1996. *The Coming Race War in America: A Wake-up Call.* Boston: Little, Brown.

Ryan, William. 1981. *Equality.* New York: Pantheon Books.

—. 1971. *Blaming the Victim.* New York: Pantheon Books.

Scruggs, L. A. 1893. *Women of Distinction Remarkable in Works and Invincible in Character.* Raleigh, N.C.: L.A. Scruggs.

Scruggs-Leftwich, Yvonne. 2006. *Consensus and Compromise Creating the First National Urban Policy under President Carter.* Lanham, Md: University Press of America.

Scruggs-Leftwich, Yvonne, and Sonia R. Jarvis. 1999. *Lift Every Voice and Vote Black Leadership Forum Operation Big Vote: A Report on Black Leaders' Successes in the 1998 Mid-term Elections through the National Non-partisan Leadership Coalition for Political Participation and Education.* [Washington, D.C.]: Black Leadership Forum.

Sleeper, Jim. 1997. *Liberal Racism*. New York: Viking.

Smiley, Tavis. 2000. *Doing What's Right: How to Fight for What You Believe and Make a Difference*. New York: Doubleday.

Thernstrom, Stephan, and Abigail M. Thernstrom. 1997. *America in Black and White: One Nation, Indivisible*. New York, NY: Simon & Schuster.

West, Cornel and Kelvin Shawn Sealey. 1997. *Restoring Hope Conversations on The Future of Black America*. Boston, Mass: Beacon Press.

West, Cornel. 1993. *Race Matters*. Boston: Beacon Press.

Wilkins, Roger W. 2001. *Jefferson's Pillow: The Founding Fathers and The Dilemma of Black Patriotism*. Boston: Beacon Press.

Wilson, William J. 1978. *The Declining Significance of Race: Blacks and Changing American Institutions*. Chicago: University of Chicago Press.

Wright, Richard, and Edwin Rosskam. 1988. *12 Million Black Voices*. New York: Thunder's Mouth Press.

Wright, Sarah E. 1990. *A. Philip Randolph Integration in The Workplace*. The History of The Civil Rights Movement. Englewood Cliffs, NJ: Silver Burdett Press.

Organizations

A. Philip Randolph Institute (APRI)
815–16th Street NW, Washington, D.C. 20006
Website: www.apri.org
APRI has influenced innumerable elections crucial to the Black-Labor Alliance and has registered and brought to the polls millions of Black voters across the nation, working in virtually every city with a sizable black population.

African American Cultural Complex (AACC)
119 Sunnybrook Road, Raleigh, N.C. 27610
Website: www.aaccmuseum.org
The African American Cultural Complex is a unique collection of artifacts, documents and displays of outstanding contributions made by African Americans and are housed in several buildings along a picturesque nature trail. The AACC currently has three exhibit houses located along a natural trail beside a creek, a mini-amphitheater, a bird sanctuary, nature preserve and a picnic area and botanical gardens.

Black Leadership Forum, Inc. (BLF)
910 17th Street NW, Washington, D.C. 20006
Website: www.blackleadershipforum.org
BLF promotes creative and coordinated Black Leadership that empowers African Americans to improve their own lives and expand their opportunities to fully participate in American social, economic and political life.

Black Women United for Action (BWUFA)
6551 Loisdale Court, Suite 218, Springfield, VA. 22150
Website: www.bwufa.org
BWUFA is a diverse, volunteer, non-profit community service

organization. Its mission is to advocate the concerns of women and improve the lives of impoverished, vulnerable families through a self-sufficiency/empowerment approach. BWUFA utilizes combined talents to provide a variety of community programs and support services through a grassroots "hands-on" method that has been effective in creating positive change.

Center for Community and Economic Justice, Inc.
Still Standing Ministry
2926 First Avenue South, St. Petersburg, FL. 33712
Website: www.still-standing.org
The Still Standing program assists men and women in achieving their recovery goals by offering access to a network of sponsors, professional therapists, experienced and recovering house managers, program coordinators, as well as faith-based guidance from Rev. Ed Leftwich. For residents in need of more clinical assistance resources such as hospitals, detoxification centers, social service agencies, churches and homeless shelters is facilitated. Still Standing is a faith-based and experienced-based program for men and women who have made the choice to recapture their lives.

Children's Defense Fund (CDF)
25 E Street NW, Washington, D.C. 20001
Website: www.childrensdefense.org
CDF began in 1973 and is a private, nonprofit organization supported by foundation and corporate grants and individual donations that has never taken government funds. CDF provides a strong, effective voice for all the children of America who cannot vote, lobby, or speak for themselves. They pay particular attention to the needs of poor and minority children and those with disabilities, and encourages preventive investment before children get sick or into trouble, drop out of school, or suffer family breakdown.

Coalition of Black Trade Unionists (CBTU)

1625 L Street NW, Washington, D.C. 20036

Website: www.cbtu.org

The CBTU consists of members from seventy-seven international and national unions with forty-two chapters across the country. CBTU's function is to improve economic development and employment opportunities for black workers; support job training initiatives and programs for black youth; work for the protection of consumers from escalating prices; and oppose cutbacks in social programs, health, welfare, aid to the cities and support services for the disadvantaged.

Congressional Black Caucus (CBC)

2236 Rayburn Building House Office Building

Washington, D.C. 20515

Website: www.congressionalblackcaucus.net

Members of the CBC represent many of the largest and most populated urban centers in the country, together with some of the most expansive and rural congressional districts in the nation. CBC members, now work as advocates for America's varied constituent interests—developing an ever-expanding legislative agenda—as well as addressing the concerns of their own particular districts.

Feminist Majority Foundation (FMF)

1600 Wilson Boulevard, Suite 801, Arlington, VA. 22209

Website: www.feminist.org

FMF is a cutting edge organization dedicated to women's equality, reproductive health, and non-violence. In all spheres, FMF utilizes research and action to empower women economically, socially, and politically. FMF believes that feminists—both women and men, girls and boys—are the majority, and that this majority must be empowered.

Georgia Coalition for the People's Agenda (The Coalition)

100 Auburn Avenue, Atlanta, GA. 30303

Website: www.gcpagenda.org

The Coalition is a body of representatives from major advocacy groups charged with programmatically addressing the concerns, needs and hopes of the People as delineated in The Agenda.

Joint Center for Political and Economic Studies (Joint Center)
1090 Vermont Avenue NW
Suite 1100, Washington, D.C. 20005
Website: www.jointcenter.org

The Joint Center is a national, nonprofit research and public policy institution recognized today as one of the nation's premier think tanks on a broad range of public policy issues of concern to African Americans and other communities of color.

National Association for the Advancement of Colored People (NAACP)
4805 Mt. Hope Drive, Baltimore, MD. 21215
Website: www.naacp.org

For nearly one hundred years NAACP has worked to ensure a society in which all individuals have equal rights and there is no racial hatred or racial discrimination.

NAACP Legal Defense Fund
and Educational Fund, Inc. (LDF)
99 Hudson Street, Suite 1600, New York, NY. 10013
Website: www.naacpldf.org

The NAACP Legal Defense and Educational Fund is America's legal counsel on issues of race. Through advocacy and litigation, LDF focuses on issues of education, voter protection, economic justice and criminal justice. We encourage students to embark on careers in the public interest through scholarship and internship programs. LDF pursues racial justice to move our nation toward a society that fulfills the promise of equality for all Americans.

National Black Business Council, Inc. (NBBC)
600 Corporate Pointe, Suite 1010, Culver City. CA, 90230
Website: www.nbbc.org
The NBBC is a non profit organization dedicated to the creation and advancement of African American and minority owned businesses. The NBBC's mission is to create and support programs that will close the economic and digital divides between minority and majority businesses.

National Black Caucus of State Legislators (NBCSL)
444 North Capitol Street, NW, Suite 622
Washington, D.C. 20001
Website: www.nbcsl.com
NBCSL is a clearinghouse and network for African American legislators and their constituents, and provides the African American community with a vital platform for access, equity and empowerment. NBCSL's unique role in America's political life has resulted in laws that govern our states and affect our daily lives.

National Coalition on Black Civic Participation, Inc.
(The National Coalition)
1900 L Street NW, Suite 700, Washington, D.C. 20036
Website: www.ncbcp.org
The National Coalition serves as an effective facilitator and convener at the local, state and national levels to fulfill the realization of a full democracy.

National Congress of Black Women, Inc. (NCBW)
1224 W Street, SE, Washington, D.C. 20020
Website: www.npcbw.org
NCBW, formerly known as The National Political Congress of Black Women, is dedicated to the educational, political, economic, and

cultural development of African American women and their families.

National Council of Negro Women (NCNW)
633 Pennsylvania Avenue, NW, Washington, D.C. 20004
Website: **www.ncnw.org**
NCNW is "an organization of organizations." NCNW represents the national and international concerns of Black women. It also gives Black women the opportunity to realize their goals for social justice and human rights through united, constructive action.

National Minority Supplier Development Council, Inc. (NMSDC) 1040 Avenue of the Americas, 2nd Floor
New York, NY. 10018
Website: **www.nmsdcus.org**
NMSDC's primary objective is to provide a direct link between corporate America and **minority-owned businesses**, and to provide increased procurement and business opportunities for minority businesses of all sizes. NMSDC is one of the country's leading business membership organizations.

National Newspaper Publishers Association (NNPA)
3200 13th Street, NW, Washington, D.C. 20010
Website: **www.nnpa.org**
NNPA, also known as the Black Press of America, is a sixty-five-year-old federation of more than 200 Black community newspapers from across the United States.

National Organization of Blacks in Government (BIG)
3005 Georgia Avenue NW, Washington, D.C. 20001
Website: **www.blacksingovernment.org**
BIG is a national response to the need for African Americans in public service to organize around issues of mutual concern and use their

collective strength to confront workplace and community issues. BIG's goals are to promote equity in all aspects of American life, excellence in public service, and opportunity for all Americans.

National Urban League, Inc. (NUL)
120 Wall Street, 8th Floor, New York, NY. 10005
Website: www.nul.org
NUL is the nation's oldest and largest community- based movement devoted to enabling African Americans to secure economic self-reliance, parity, power and civil rights.

Operation Hope, Inc. (OHI)
707 Wilshire Boulevard, Suite 3030, Los Angeles, CA 90017
Website: www.operationhope.org
OHI is a public benefit organization, founded immediately following the civil unrest of April 29, 1992 in Los Angeles. OHI is America's leading provider of economic tools and services, and is an effective facilitator, lender, advocate and educator for and on behalf of the other America.

Opportunities Industrialization Centers of America, Inc. (OICA) 1415 North Broad Street, Philadelphia, PA 19122
Website: www.oicofamerica.org
OICA prepares people for today's workforce with quality life skills development, fundamental education, superior job skills training, and employment readiness services. OICA has sixty affiliates in thirty states across the country and the District of Columbia.

RainbowPUSH Coalition (RainbowPUSH)
930 East 50th Street, Chicago, IL 60615
Website: www.rainbowpush.org
The RainbowPUSH Coalition is a mighty coalition of progressive men and women of many races and cultures who have banded together to

fight for social change. RainbowPUSH is a combination of grassroots and political organizations merged together, that seek to protect, defend and gain civil rights and to even the economic and educational playing fields in all aspects of American life and to bring peace to the world

Sojourner Truth Forum for Interactive Justice
P. O. Box 10505, St. Petersburg, FL. 33730
Website: www.yscruggs.com
Executive Director, Dr. Yvonne Scruggs-Leftwich

Southern Christian Leadership Conference (SCLC)
One Georgia Center—600 West Peachtree Street
9th Floor, Atlanta, GA. 30308
Website: www.sclcnational.org
The SCLC is a nonprofit, non-sectarian, inter-faith, advocacy organization that is committed to non-violent action to achieve social, economic, and political justice. In the spirit of Dr. Martin Luther King, Jr, the SCLC is committed to bring about the promise of "one nation, under God, indivisible" together with the commitment to activate the "strength to love" within the community of humankind.

100 Black Men of America, Inc.
141 Auburn Avenue, Atlanta, GA. 30303
Website: www.100blackmen.org
The mission of the 100 Black Men of America, Inc. is to improve the quality of life within our communities and enhance educational and economic opportunities for all African Americans. We are committed to the intellectual development of youth and the economic empowerment of the African American community based on the following precepts: respect for family, spirituality, justice, and integrity.

Index

J

Jackson, Jesse, L., 81
Jackson Lee, Sheila, 13
Jarrett, Vernon, vi
Johnson, Eddie, Bernice, 12
Johnson, Jeffalyn, 29
Johns, Marie, C., 38
Johnson, George, A., 86
Joint Center for Political and Economic Studies, 29, 36, 43, 46, 81, 83, 108, 112, 120, 122, 136
Jones, Ingrid Saunders, 38
Jones, Phillip, E., vi
Jones, Stephanie Tubbs, 17
Jordan, June, vi, xv
Jordan, Vernon, 63, 82

K

Kerner Commission (Report), 120, 129, 131
Kilpatrick, Carolyn, 16–17
King, Coretta Scott, 37, 64, 146
King, Jr., Martin, L., vi, 37, 98, 103–104, 129, 144, 146
King, Rodney, 74

L

Lanier, Bob, 109
Lawyers Committee for Civil Rights, 32
Lee, Barbara, 17
Lieberman, Joseph, 34
Lightfoot, Sara Lawrence, 136
Lind, Michael, 95–96
Locke, Alain Leroy, 73, 100
Lord Byron, 79
Lowery, Joseph, E., 64, 81–82

M

Madhubuti, Haki, R., vi
Marshall, Thurgood, 75
Marx, Karl, 93
McKinney, Cynthia, A., 15

Wilkins, Roy, 37
Williams, Eddie, N., 63, 81, 83
Williams, Patricia, vi
Wilson, William Julius, 119, 136
       The Declining Significance of Race, 136
Winston, Judith, 94
Women for Human Rights and Dignity, 24–25, 28
Women's History Month, 35
Woodson, Carter, G., 35, 91
World Conference Against Racism (WCAR), 13, 71–72, 75
Wright, Elizabeth Evelyn, 105–106, 111–115

Y
Young, Whitney, 37
Young Women's Christian Association (YWCA), 3
Yoo, John, 107
Ylvisaker, Dean Paul, vi

Printed in the United States
201982BV00003B/130-231/P